Praise for the original
1994 *Postpartum Survival Guide:*

Without talking down to their readers, Dunnewold and Sanford empathetically address the less acknowledged negative side of new parenthood, offering tools and strategies that really help them solve problems and confidently take on the parenting role.
-Penny Simkin, coauthor of *Pregnancy, Childbirth, and the Newborn* and *The Simple Guide to Having a Baby*

A woman and her family can be healthier both emotionally and physically because of the practical advice, personal insight, and honesty of *Postpartum Survival Guide.*
-Jane Honikman, Founder, Postpartum Support International

Goes beyond most self-help titles in addressing a range of special contemporary issues, from the challenges facing single and older mothers to adoptive mothers and those who have become mothers only after much struggle. Fathers, too, are included in the discussions, which feature exercises to aid recovery.
-The Bookwatch, **November 1994**

Publisher's Note:

This publication is designed to provide accurate and authoritative information in regard to the subject matter covered. It is sold with the understanding that neither the publisher nor authors intend this work to render psychological, financial, legal, or other professional services. This work is educational in nature, with no warranties or guarantees indirectly or explicitly implied. It is not intended to replace medical or psychological services of any kind. If expert assistance or counsel is needed, the services of a competent professional should be sought.

DEDICATION:

To our husbands, Randy and Steve, who've supported our relentless commitment to improving the emotional health of pregnant and postpartum women. Also, to the women who have shared their stories and lives with us: you make it all worthwhile.

ISBN: 978-0-982-64100-2

Life Will Never Be The Same: The Real Mom's Postpartum Survival Guide

Ann Dunnewold, Ph.D. and
Diane Sanford, Ph.D.

with foreword by Gladys Tse, M.D.

Real Moms Ink, LLC

Contents

FOREWORD

Most people don't know this about me, but I carry a full obstetric delivery kit in the trunk of my car. I do this because as an obstetrician, resident, and medical student, I have delivered babies on planes, in airports and in bedrooms. I have tied off and cut umbilical cords with so many unpredictable things that I now have learned to be prepared. Unfortunately, this façade of preparedness, this management of the unknown, sometimes still fails me. I find myself kneeling in front of a laboring woman in an unfamiliar place, yet again, without a pair of gloves. I share this with you because I think that all of us, as women, ultimately feel this way about new motherhood. Despite all of our planning, we still find ourselves ill-equipped to deal with the hormonal, emotional and real-life changes that are thrust upon us.

The history of obstetrics is full of drama and magic. A few hundred years ago, obstetrical instruments such as forceps were coated with leather and hidden within the confines of the ubiquitous white coat so as not to "alarm the mother" with the clanging noise. Deliveries were done beneath a white sheet, and little was communicated about the process. Medications like scopolamine and twilight furthered the secrecy. This secrecy has largely been eliminated and replaced by modern tools of obstetrical empowerment: birth plans and informed consent. Despite this, while obstetricians have involved future mothers and fathers in virtually every aspect of childbirth leading up to the blessed event, we are remarkably reticent regarding issues of ante-partum and postpartum depression, guilt and anxiety. We hesitate for the same reasons we hid our forceps in our coats, for fear of alarming our patients, a fear that is fed by modern myths and misunderstanding. Although we are adept at citing the alarming statistics that up to 89% of all new mothers will feel postpartum blues and that up to 20% of these women will develop postpartum depression, we remain less confident at equipping our patients with tools to cope with the enormous life upheaval that is new motherhood.

Preparation must necessarily involve communication. There are legitimate and real hormonal changes that can explain the feelings of fear and anxiety in the early postpartum period. Estrogen and progesterone, hormones that had previously maintained the pregnancy, decline to their lowest levels immediately after birth. This emotional, hormonally charged effect can last for weeks and sometimes even months. Researchers at Yale University have documented MRI findings that show how a new mother's brain response to her baby's cry mimics that of a deeply anxious patient. It is thought that this heightened sense of anxiety carries with it an evolutionary protection: it is the body's most dynamic way of communicating that something is wrong and propelling it to act. In moderation, this transient anxiety can move a new mom to connect with her baby. But if it becomes excessive, the anxiety can lead to detachment, apathy and depression. Discussion with your obstetrician can open the lines of communication and help you to be better equipped for the ever-changing road ahead.

Postpartum depression has been misunderstood for centuries. Two thousand years ago, Hippocrates believed that new mothers went mad because their breast milk was diverted to their brains. Today, Tom Cruise rants that "psychiatry is a pseudo-science, there is no such thing as a chemical imbalance in the body." Brooke Shields' disclosure that she suffered from and was treated for postpartum depression has prompted invaluable honesty, dispelling the myth that new motherhood is 100% elation. The elation fantasy leaves postpartum women vulnerable and alone, feeling as though they are deficient or bad mothers.

In spite of excellent planning and preparation, some women will still suffer from some form of postpartum depression. As I mentioned in the first paragraph, there are always situations that no amount of planning can prevent. In these instances, it is important to have resources and strategies to combat these common feelings of hopelessness and worthlessness, to start the road to recovery.

This is a book after my own heart. Despite all attempts at preparedness and planning, I acknowledge one simple truth about life, and of course, about motherhood: It is a unique experience for each and every person and is always filled with peaks and valleys, ups and downs. Early identification and rapid treatment are essential to recovery from postpartum depression. As clinicians, we know that the number and severity of consequences increases with the duration of the depression. As women, we should support each other in the fight towards universal acceptance of pregnancy and childbirth as a life changing event, one that is best never travelled alone. Use this wonderful book as your guide and your strength.

Gladys Tse, M.D.
Assistant Professor, Obstetrics and Gynecology
Director, Resident Surgical Education
Washington University in Saint Louis

1

Motherhood:
The Most Demanding Job, Ever

Having a baby is supposed to mark one of the happiest times in your life. For nine months, you await your baby's birth with a whole range of emotions, from nervous anticipation to endless joy. Society is quite clear about what your emotions are supposed to be when your baby is born. Television, movies, magazines, and newspapers all give you the message that happiness, satisfaction, joy, and pride are the norm when a new baby arrives. Family, friends, and medical professionals tell you to "relax and enjoy your baby," as if relaxation played even the smallest role in the drama of life with a brand-new child.

Hardly anyone talks about the enormous physical, emotional, and relationship changes which accompany the birth of a new baby. Maybe it's because no one wants to be the killjoy sounding notes of grim reality amid all the soft-focus hype. But for many women and their families, the experience of having a baby turns out differently from their expectations. You may feel devastated when all your beautiful images of motherhood crash into a pile at your feet. "It wasn't supposed to be like this," you want to shake your fist and shout at someone. And the worst part of it is that no one *really* wants to listen. Even the eyes of your closest sister may glaze over when negative words come out of your mouth. When you report that you're so sleep-deprived that you feel like an eighty-year-old running a marathon, well-meaning friends and health professionals will tell you to sleep when your baby sleeps. Who do they think they're kidding? When their babies sleep, new mothers soak their episiotomy stitches, or throw some food in the oven, or agonize over the birth announcements they haven't even had time to buy, much less address the envelopes.

The reality is that becoming a parent is a considerable task. The new mother's body appears to have gone haywire. Her hormones fluctuate daily. She is suffering from sleep deprivation; she's tired beyond belief. (Sleep deprivation, by the way, is a tried-and-true method for torturing prisoners of war!) The new mother is physically vulnerable from hormone shifts and the enormous physical stress of childbirth. After a couple days' rest, if she's lucky, she is put in charge of meeting another human being's needs before tending to any of her own. Feed the baby, diaper the baby, rock and walk the baby, wash all the clothes that the baby spit up on, and try to squeeze in her own shower or lunch, let alone fun. That's without even considering work, in or out of the home.

On top of these physical changes are emotional changes. You are now someone's mother, with the entire psychological burden that role carries in society. Having to put your child's needs first means that every other role you have played must be revised — partner, daughter, friend, worker. You suddenly end up on the bottom of the list, after all the pampering and praise of pregnancy. You may quite naturally feel exhausted, unsure, and overwhelmed. Because of the cultural myth of "this wonderful time," your negative feelings may have taken you completely by surprise. Since it wasn't supposed to be like this, you may find yourself feeling angry, cheated, and depressed. Who wouldn't, when you discover that the bliss and well-being you expected have been buried under overwhelming worry and exhaustion?

What is most important to remember is that these negative feelings make sense when you look at the task a new mother must tackle. When you lack sleep, you are going to feel exhausted. When you take on a new job, it's normal to feel scared and uncertain. When you have little time to take care of your own need for fun, companionship, and order, it's logical that you feel frustrated, resentful, and overwhelmed. Yet few resources for new mothers include a discussion of these negative feelings, or warn you about what to expect emotionally in the postpartum period. Instead, the myth of maternal bliss endures, leaving many women feeling depressed and ashamed.

A New View of Motherhood

Our culture romanticizes motherhood and fosters many unrealistic expectations, often leaving women feeling as if they have failed. Rather than rejecting society's expectations as unrealistic, women tend to see themselves as the problem. One mother told us, "When I thought of becoming a mother, I pictured myself singing to my baby and walking her in her stroller—happy all the time, thoroughly enjoying being a mom. When that didn't happen, I blamed myself. I looked at my daughter, certain that someone else could take better care of her than I could. Someone else would know what to do. I kept thinking that maybe I didn't deserve to have this baby. Yet all my life I had wanted to be a mom. What was wrong with me?" To prevent postpartum problems and deal with them effectively, society must embrace a new view of motherhood, one that recognizes the period following childbirth as a time of tremendous physical, emotional, and interpersonal upheaval. Although having a child can be joyful in many ways, it also involves enormous challenge and change.

Our new view of motherhood has to be more real, more accurate. We need to recognize that being a mother is the most demanding job you will ever do. The tremendous rewards of motherhood are not minimized or forgotten. But more emphasis needs to be placed on the challenges that are part of the territory. Cultural bias often minimizes the job. You are adopting this attitude yourself if you ever degrade yourself by saying, "I am just a mom." We need to recognize the critical importance *and* the stress of being a parent. Motherhood is not always the glowing and rewarding job it appears to be on television and in magazines. Parenting is tough work. Being a mother is being in the trenches, mucking out the stalls, completing tasks that are neither glorious nor immediately satisfying. You just can't keep going if you neglect your own need for rest, fun, and order and control in your life.

Society (and those around the new mother) needs to support mothers more, validating the importance of the job. Good mothering is not only immensely valuable but also essential to a healthy society. We need to recognize that mothers (and fathers) are fallible human beings. Many people have difficulty adjusting to their new jobs as parents. *All* parents deserve society's support and gratitude. Validation of the hard work of motherhood can make women feel freer to admit when it is difficult. You can take pride in the job of parenthood when you allow yourself to see what a significant contribution it is! It does not matter if your child becomes a truck driver or a judge. If you have a hand in producing a well-rounded, functioning member of society, you have done **good work**.

What makes this new job so demanding? Step back a moment and look at some of the realities of the day- to-day job itself:

o   **Parenting is nonstop**. As a mother, you are always on duty. You are even on call when your child is sleeping. In a paid job, labor laws in this country require that you sit down for two twenty-minute breaks and a thirty-minute lunch during an eight-hour shift. If life with a new baby has three eight-hour shifts a day, you are entitled to breaks totaling three and a half hours per day. Multiply that by seven days, and you deserve nearly 25 hours off!

o   **Parenting is drudgery.** Repetitive, mindless, physical labor is what childcare is about, particularly in infancy. Change diapers, wipe spit up, do laundry, walk a squalling sack of potatoes around for hours on end. It is important to remember that you can love the child and hate the job. A recent survey that asked mothers to rate the enjoyment from their daily activities placed childcare below nearly every activity — slightly more satisfying only than housework, paid work, and commuting. Big picture, mothers do realize that there are sweet and satisfying moments laced within the drudgery — at least eventually.

o   **There are few absolute answers about how to parent correctly.** No matter how hard you try to do right by your child, you are absolutely guaranteed to make some mistakes. Everyone from Grandma to the pediatrician has ready advice, solicited or not. Everyone has a better way. Even the experts often give conflicting advice. Since there is no single "right" way, you will have to define what works for you. Expect to make, and overcome, your share of mistakes.

o   **Society devalues the job of parenting.** As a culture, we don't honor the job of motherhood, especially financially. Unlike some nations, we don't guarantee paid parental leave. We pay childcare workers and teachers minimal wages to replace parents. If you have ever watched the face of a new acquaintance at a party when you announce you are "just a mom," you know this is true. We recognize mothers one day per year — Mother's Day.

o **Society devalues the intensity of the job.** Again, our culture doesn't attribute much importance to the job of motherhood because we simply don't think it is very hard. Not only do we not value the contributions of mothers, but we also have trouble as a society believing that parenting is really any big deal. Any thirteen-year-old can do it, no license required. So if you are having a tough time, getting frustrated, irritable, fatigued, or angry, the message says "there must be something wrong with you." Validation — that it is exhausting, demanding, challenging, even crazy-making hard work — is not universally forthcoming.

o **Return on your investment is slow.** As a mother, your product will not be finished for a long time — eighteen or more years, to be sure. You even have to wait two months to see a smile. Human beings plod along a bit easier when they get positive feedback on how they are performing; this is why most employers have yearly job evaluations. Raising a child lacks that feedback, and so the job is even more difficult — how can you know you are on the right track? This leads us to the final factor.

o **Parenthood is one of the most important jobs there is. Period.** This is one of the most critical undertakings you will engage in across your lifetime, and our culture says your value (and the value of the human being you are launching) is on the line. If your child misbehaves, makes bad choices, or can't measure up, this society we live in will point the finger at you. This fault-finding is patently unfair, for there are myriad influences on a child's development. Most parents struggle with this pressure nonetheless.

Adopting a more balanced view of motherhood may help women stop blaming themselves for their struggles postpartum and beyond! If the period following childbirth is expected to be difficult, and the job of motherhood is accepted as challenging, women may see their problems as part of a normal adjustment process, rather than as personal shortcomings. They may feel more comfortable asking for assistance from family and friends and speaking up when problems occur rather than suffering in silence. A change in society's attitude may give women permission to be more loving and gentle toward themselves as they learn to be moms and to appreciate the persistence that parenting requires. When it's accepted that you are taking on a challenge, you (and those around you) can more easily see the necessity for taking care of yourself, emotionally as well as physically. Self-preservation, rather than total self-sacrifice, becomes the standard.

A second incorrect belief is the assumption that mother-knowledge somehow occurs spontaneously when a woman gives birth. Although mothering is biologically programmed to a minor extent, it is mostly a learning process. Just as it takes time and practice to become an accomplished musician, it takes time and practice to learn to be a perfectly good mom. Why doesn't society reinforce this message? Women are taught to believe that they are somehow supposed to know what to do—from changing diapers to choosing preschools—from the moment their child is born. And they are expected to do it well—if not perfectly! The pressure of this expectation can be crushing. How can you ask for help about something you "should" already know? What if someone else catches you making a mistake? Your ignorance or uncertainty then becomes an occasion for shame—just one more reason to feel bad about yourself.

When society acknowledges that mothering is a learning process, many new attitudes can flourish. Women can be more patient with themselves, because everyone knows that learning a new skill takes time. Mistakes can become opportunities to learn something new, rather than ammunition for self-contempt. Less experienced moms may be more likely to get assistance and advice from the best teachers of all: moms who have been through it all before. Shame and blame will diminish about what you don't know. Learning, instead of knowing, will be the operative word.

Finally, there is the Supermom myth to challenge. This myth implies that there is some single, right way to be a good mom. It suggests that one style of mothering is better than all others, and that anyone who falls short of this ideal is made of inferior goods. The image of Supermom has changed as often as hemlines. These days,

Supermom is loving but firm. She listens, then acts. She's sensitive but in control. Supermom of the Millennium is supportive but encourages independence. She's informed and active, attentive to her children's needs. She nurtures her own needs as well. She's involved, soft, strong, capable, and mature. She's an emotional giant. She always knows the right thing to do and does it all perfectly. Whether she stays at home or works outside her home, her life is totally in order. She never misses a beat. She is the standard of success. Hers is the image to which many women compare themselves. No wonder they feel so bad!

Telling yourself that you have to be Supermom is like telling yourself that you need to look like a high-fashion model: it's possible, given the right natural endowments, but it's not realistic for most of us. It's ridiculous and self-destructive to hold yourself to such impossibly high standards. Society must let go of the notion that there is only one way to be a good mom. Motherhood is an extremely complicated role—so complex, in fact, that achieving perfection and always being right are simply impossible. Every mother makes mistakes, because mothers are only human.

There are many functional, loving approaches to motherhood. It is up to each woman to develop her own style and to follow her heart. When society promotes diversity, there will be no shame in not conforming to one particular ideal. Women will be able to feel self-esteem and self-acceptance because they have differences, sprung from an individual vision of what is right and good. Each woman can define her own model for mothering and drop self-blame for falling short of some unattainable ideal.

Given this demanding job of motherhood, you need to give yourself a break emotionally. If you were undertaking any other equally stressful job, you would allow time to learn what you need to know. As a popular new baby card quips, you will encounter joy, wonder, *and* lack of sleep.

The Wide Range of "Normal" Postpartum Adjustment

We want to educate women and their families about the wide range of feelings that are possible after the birth of a baby. This book was written for two reasons. Reason number one is to let you know that having a baby is a tough adjustment: feeling lost or down or nervous is as understandable (and as likely) as tears of joy when you gaze upon your sleeping infant. After accepting that, reason number two naturally follows: if this immense, demanding job looms ahead of you, learning to take care of yourself will be key to surviving and thriving in the job. We want not only to firmly burn into your brain the necessity of tending to your own needs; we also want to teach you how to balance self-care with the demands of a family.

When you ask women what their postpartum adjustment period is like, you will hear a wide range of answers. Some new mothers feel wonderful, in charge, and confident. Some feel giddily in love, obsessed with this new being. Others report feeling just plain rotten. Look at this list of feelings mentioned by women in a new mothers' group:

"I am so irritable. I am full of awe. I cry all the time. I can't sleep. I am so in love. I can't get going. I can't think straight. I feel so worried. I am so bored. I can't feel anything. I have scary thoughts. I am ecstatic. I grieve for my old life. I feel like a failure. I feel so alone. I feel so nervous. I feel obsessed with the baby. I feel I've made a huge mistake."

We understand how difficult such a mix of feelings can be when you expected a glowing life. We know, first as women and mothers and then as psychologists, the sense of guilt and failure when having that new baby in your life feels less than wonderful. In our work as psychologists, we've seen the relief in women's faces when their negative feelings are validated. Women feel crazy for having negative feelings. They feel deficient and abnormal and ashamed. If it were possible to put a big motherly hug into words, that's what we'd do for every postpartum mom who opens this book. In the words of Jane Honikman, founder of Postpartum Support International, we want you to know that you are not alone, you are not to blame, and you can feel better.

Why do you hear so little about negative postpartum emotions? Part of the answer is that society still wants to believe that new motherhood is nothing but wonderful. Women who have negative feelings in the postpartum period are afraid to talk. They feel as if something is wrong with them or that they'll be rejected by family or friends if they come clean about how they feel. They may not want to scare or worry other new mothers. This, combined with shame for their negative feelings, means that postpartum mothers don't even confide very much about their worst fears to other women. But a look at the statistics confirms how common postpartum reactions are. Researchers often find widely varied answers when they poll new mothers about their feelings. Generally, however, it appears that from fifty to eighty percent of all new mothers experience some short-lived negative feelings that can be classified as "the blues." Probably ten to twenty percent of new mothers have longer-lasting and more upsetting bouts of negative feelings. Postpartum depression, anxiety, obsessive-compulsive, and panic clinical conditions fall in this range, with ten to twenty new mothers out of every one hundred experiencing some of these difficulties. Finally, only one or two out of every one thousand new mothers actually experiences the most extreme clinical condition: postpartum psychosis.

A Guide To Feeling Better

Realizing that the feelings you have are neither uncommon nor your fault is only the first step toward feeling better. Our second goal is to give you some tools to help you feel well emotionally and, in turn, to prevent postpartum depression and anxiety. Finally, we offer strategies to manage your feelings and improve the quality of your postpartum life. In our work as psychologists, we've counseled hundreds of women who struggled with their feelings and behaviors after having a baby. From these women, we've learned a great deal about what works. Support is important. So is the knowledge that this is the most demanding job you will encounter, that you are neither alone nor the first person to feel this way. However, you also need to take care of yourself. We agree with Ellen McGrath, Ph.D., chair of an American Psychological Association task force on women and depression. McGrath says listening and talking are not enough. As Dr. McGrath prescribes, you must act for things to change.

The process of feeling better begins with letting go of the myth that you will only feel wonderful after the birth of your baby. Next you must relinquish the self-blame, the idea that you are deficient or inadequate if you don't feel ecstatic. You can then tune into your own needs and the location of your anguish. What do you need most of all? How can you balance your own needs and the needs of those who are important to you, from the baby to other family members? What do your reactions — the negative feelings or behaviors you have — tell you about issues you need to tackle? When you know what your needs are, you can begin to develop a plan to meet those needs. You can learn a new habit of taking care of yourself. We believe taking care of yourself is critical to your physical and psychological health. It is also an essential skill in becoming a caring and successful parent.

Think of yourself as a pitcher of water. Every time you give to someone, meeting his or her needs, you are pouring water out of that pitcher. If you rock the baby, you are meeting her need for comfort. A little water pours out of your pitcher. You listen to your partner's report of a frustrating day. That takes a bit more from your pitcher. You take the baby for her checkup, draining the pitcher a bit more. You talk to a friend who had a big fight with her husband. By offering support, you are depleting your pitcher once again. The catch is that you are not a bottomless pitcher. You must stop at some point and do something to fill the pitcher again. And how do you fill your pitcher? You take care of yourself.

You can learn what works best to refill your pitcher. Some people like to relax in a hot bath, while others prefer exercising, or reading funny stories, or talking with supportive and nurturing friends. No matter what you do to fill the pitcher, it is essential that you do something. When you give and give without paying attention to your own needs, you're in danger of draining yourself dry. This book takes you through the steps of replenishment within the context of the normal, but nonetheless extraordinary, demands of new motherhood. We also provide concrete guidelines about when you need more help than you can provide for yourself and how and where you can get such assistance.

Using This Book

We know that one of your biggest postpartum problems is finding enough time to take care of your most basic needs. Taking a shower, buying and preparing food, then stealing a few moments to stuff it into your mouth (to say nothing of trying to get a few hours of uninterrupted sleep) can all seem monumental. Believe us. We've been there. Reading probably isn't very high on your list of priorities right now. If you're breastfeeding your baby, you might be able to squeeze some reading time into your nursing sessions. Even with bottle-feeding, you may be able to juggle the book and the bottle if you use a bookstand, such as one that would hold a cookbook open. If you're lucky enough to have a baby who sleeps a lot—or you have a baby who nurses almost constantly—reading may already be part of your routine. To make the most efficient use of whatever reading time you do have, we've written a short summary at the beginning of each chapter. Read this if you don't have time for anything else. Each summary contains a suggestion for coping — either an easy-to-do exercise or a behavioral or attitudinal change.

You might want to keep this book by the chair where you most often feed or nurse your baby. Read further as time allows; focus on the chapters that best fit your needs. Stick the book in the diaper bag when you go out. Look at a few more pages as you wait to see the pediatrician or your physician, or as you wait in line at the bank drive-through. Making time for reading this book is one of the first steps in taking care of yourself. Setting aside ten minutes, morning or evening, and exploring the ideas contained here can be a great investment in your health. If you take a little time to do something for yourself, you will find a payback in terms of having more energy and a better frame of mind.

Words of Encouragement and Hope

By now, you may be feeling some relief and hope that you can get beyond the postpartum period by either preventing or surviving a true crisis. Facing up to the fact that this time in your life has not been exactly what you expected is the first step. Letting go of the guilt about that is the second. Embracing the reality of the demanding job, complete with drudgery and pressure, can feel like a relief. You don't need to apologize to anyone about taking care of yourself once you accept the critical role of self-care for all moms. You may feel a lot of anxiety and uncertainty about whether you can succeed, for your life these days may feel like a failure. Listen carefully: you deserve credit for having the strength to tackle the difficulties of your life during this transitional time. Pat yourself on the back. You can do it. The act of picking up this book and reading this far is proof that you have the resources needed to make things better.

As you approach the task of becoming a mom, you need to have realistic expectations. In our clinical work, we've learned that the process of adjustment and recovery is slow and difficult at times. It is always two steps forward, then one step back. You cannot take these suggestions and put them to work perfectly, with magical results. You are a human being, imperfect like everyone else, and cannot do everything you need to make yourself feel better every day. If you manage to persevere two days out of seven, then three days, and four, hooray for you! But if you expect every day to go well, you'll certainly be disappointed. There are always good days mixed with the bad, even under the best of circumstances. Just remember that the bad days don't mean that you've lost all your hard-won progress. When those days come, accept them as inevitable, and recognize them as survivable. They are not the result of a flaw in you, but a product of this demanding job. Focus on the progress you're making. Keep in mind that you are not alone, you are not to blame, and you will get better.

2

Self-Care: The Key to Postpartum Emotional Health

The Short Version
(If You're Pressed for Time)

The first step in feeling well after your baby arrives is to take care of yourself. Implement steps to take care of yourself *right now*, whether you are pregnant or postpartum. If you do not take care of yourself, you cannot give your baby the best care. Not only will you be more easily frustrated, irritable, and self-critical, you may be setting yourself up for a postpartum clinical condition.

The following suggestions can be included in every new mother's (or father's) plan for self-care:

o Take care of yourself physically. Get enough rest, eat right, exercise.

o Develop a support system. Make sure you have other new parents to talk to and make a point of talking to them or seeing them at least once a week.

o Express and accept your negative feelings. It's normal to feel bad sometimes when you're adjusting to a new baby. You are still an okay person even if you don't always feel constantly wonderful about this new addition to your life.

o Focus on your positive feelings. Look for ways in which you do feel good and pay attention to those too.

o Take breaks by yourself, with your partner, or with another adult. No one can work at a job nonstop without some time off every day.

o   Keep your expectations realistic. No one can do it all, let alone do it perfectly. Work toward reasonable, achievable goals, whether dealing with your feelings, the cleanliness of your home, the baby's schedule, losing your baby weight, or whatever other issues are important to you now.

o   Nurture your sense of humor. There is great value in keeping in touch with the funny side of life. Try to laugh daily, whether at yourself, your situation, or something outside of all this.

o   Structure your day. Plan loosely how you will spend your day, designating time for all the items on this list. Plan for when you will talk to another adult, when you will rest, when you will take a break. Keep the plan flexible and realistic so you can stick to it.

o   Postpone other major life changes; your life is full of enough change and stress right now as it is. Avoid taking on a new job, a new home, a new partner until you feel more settled in your new role of mother.

Exercise:
Two Minutes for Yourself

Take out a sheet of paper. Fold it in half length-wise. On one side, write your strengths. Then flip it over and write, "The mom I want to be" on the other side at the top. List the ten qualities that you think make a good mom. Your list may include virtues such as patience, drive, and organization, or more diverse elements such as playfulness or an affectionate nature. Now take a deep breath and review the lists. Which qualities do you intrinsically possess? Many of these attributes may already be on your strengths list. Circle the matching ones on both lists. Recopy these (or the top five, if you have more than five) onto a three-by-five note card with the heading "Qualities I have which make me a good mom." Tear up the other list and throw it away. Rather than fretting about what personal aspects of a stereotypic good mom you lack, focus on the strengths you bring to this new relationship. There are as many ways to be a good mother as there are opinions about getting a baby to sleep through the night. Put the card in your purse or wallet and review it regularly to build your confidence in this new role.

2

Self-Care: The Key to Postpartum Emotional Health

You are committed to doing the best for yourself and this baby in the postpartum adjustment period, just as you did throughout your pregnancy. Preventing postpartum emotional difficulties is a high priority for you. There are three key aspects to this prevention: 1) practicing physical and emotional self-care; 2) coping with normal symptoms to keep them from turning into full-fledged problems, and 3) addressing factors which might increase your risk. This chapter begins by taking you step-by-step through the process of making a self-care plan, the key to preventing postpartum emotional problems. In fact, this is not just a postpartum survival plan. This is a motherhood survival plan, the key to self-care across your lifetime. It's hard to imagine a time in a woman's life in which these ideas would not be useful. Think about starting this habit of self-care now, and expect to practice it throughout your life.

Because of biology, psychology, and relationship factors, some women will be more likely than others to experience postpartum problems. You may have been drawn to this book because you've experienced postpartum problems in the past or are experiencing them now. You sense that it is difficult to ride out as big a physical change as pregnancy and birth without some psychological impact — not just because it is a major leap to being a mother, but because your hormones work that way. You just want to be prepared, so here is the plan.

The Foundation of Motherhood Survival: Making a Self-Care Plan

Is Your Pitcher Empty or Full?

Take a deep breath, and repeat out loud: "My baby needs a mommy, not a martyr!" Taking care of yourself physically is just as important postpartum as it is when you are pregnant. While pregnant, you devoted lots of energy to doing all you could to ensure a healthy baby. Self-care now is just as essential to being the best mother you can be as was taking vitamins, exercising, and getting regular prenatal care while you were pregnant.

To be a good mother, you must be good to yourself first, both physically and emotionally. This does not mean, of course, that it's okay to neglect your baby's essential needs for food, warmth, cleanliness, or comfort. Babies are very effective when it comes to making sure that their needs are known. Screaming at 4 a.m., for instance, conveys a pretty clear message: "I need something." What you want to aim for is a balance between your own needs and those of your child. It's best to tackle this issue now, because it's one that you'll be facing for the rest of your life.

As we've noted before, a pitcher of water provides a clear demonstration of what we mean. Imagine again that you are a pitcher of water. You keep pouring out, giving and giving as you take care of the needs of those around you: baby, partner, family, friends. If you do not take action to fill the pitcher up again, pretty soon it will be empty.

No one is a bottomless pitcher. What do you need in order to fill up the pitcher again?

Permission for Self-Care

Every new mother needs to establish the habit of taking care of herself during the hectic days, weeks, and months following the birth of her baby. Many of us have buried this innate need to take care of ourselves. We think it is selfish to do things for ourselves. But if we want to have the energy for our lives, we need to keep our pitchers full. Make a conscious effort to extend this basic consideration to yourself, just as you do for others in your life. Give yourself permission for this most basic self-care, laying the groundwork for this important new habit right now.

Practice making time to do what you want to do. Learn to say no. Put some time for you on your 'to do' list. Set 30 minutes aside each day, close your door, and allow no one to interrupt you. Let your partner cook dinner. Turn off your phone and computer. Delegate responsibilities to other family members. The choices are limitless. Whatever you choose, don't back down because other things seem more pressing. Keep telling yourself, "I count. I am important. I will treat myself with care." Self-sacrifice accomplishes little beyond wearing you out, and it leaves you resentful about fulfilling other people's needs.

The Basics

It is never too late to benefit from a good self-care plan. In fact, the steps described here may just as easily be called a "parenthood survival plan." The groundwork for your motherhood survival plan should include the following elements. Strive to incorporate these elements:

o   Nurture yourself physically
o   Develop a support system
o   Express and accept negative feelings, while also attending to positive feelings
o   Take breaks
o   Keep your expectations realistic
o   Nurture your sense of humor
o   Structure your day
o   Postpone major life changes

These elements are all discussed in detail below.

Nurture yourself physically. It's absolutely essential to your physical and mental health that you take care of your physical needs. You need to get adequate sleep and rest. You need to eat properly. Vitamin supplements are important, but they're not a cure for loading up on junk food. Ask your healthcare provider for the most recent recommendations on nutrition.

Recent research on the effects of food on hormonal balance and mood suggests supplements that may help prevent or balance mood difficulties during the postpartum period. These ideas have been helpful to many women in clinical practice as well as in controlled research studies. However, this is not medical advice. Certain individuals may want to avoid some of these supplements. *Always check with your own healthcare provider before beginning any dietary or vitamin recommendations*. You may want to consider these options:

- Take 600 milligrams of calcium in the morning and 600 milligrams of calcium in the evening. Calcium may improve the metabolism of stress hormones and increase the efficiency of neurotransmitters (i.e., brain hormones) such as serotonin.
- Take 500 to 750 milligrams of magnesium per day. Magnesium is a relaxant and a natural antidepressant. Calcium and magnesium must be in a balanced, two to one ratio, e.g. 600 milligrams of calcium to every 300 milligrams of magnesium. Over-the-counter magnesium is found primarily in 250 milligram tablets, so this dose is an approximation.
- Take one gram (1000 milligrams) of omega 3 essential fatty acids (DHA and EPA) per day. Look for fish sources that specify "mercury free."
- Make sure vitamin B6 and zinc are present in your prenatal vitamin, or add a supplement of each.
- Reduce or eliminate consumption of aspartame (Nutrasweet), caffeine, processed sugar, and alcohol.
- Eat small meals every two to three hours for stability of brain hormone and blood sugar levels. Snack size portions are all you need.
- A diet rich in vegetable protein and complex carbohydrates may boost levels of the brain hormone serotonin. Soy products, whole grains, nuts, and legumes all may produce a sense of calm and well-being in persons prone to mood swings. Snack on so-called 'good carbs' frequently, such as whole wheat bagels, almonds, beans and rice, soy milk, or peanut butter on wheat crackers. Animal protein need not be avoided, but some research suggests that the amino acids in animal protein can compete with serotonin production, resulting in mood swings. Avoid animal protein (eggs, milk, cheese, yogurt, chicken, steak) by itself. Always have some carbohydrates or vegetable protein; the amino acids in these

can boost serotonin production. This can be as simple as a handful of peanuts or whole wheat crackers with your glass of milk.

Physical exercise is the third aspect of this basic foundation. The benefits of aerobic exercise are well known for losing those unwanted pounds and toning up. Increasing your activity level by exercising can provide great stress relief and raise your spirits. Look for a postpartum exercise class (where babies may be welcome). Talking with other moms who have new babies provides the added benefit of social support. Having this support is a real hedge against negative feelings.

Develop a support system. Be sure that you have a strong social support system. Having other people to depend on for emotional and practical support will reduce your stress. Speak with family and friends about how they can help you postpartum. Be direct with members of your support system about the kinds of help you will appreciate after the baby is born. Research has shown that you benefit most from support if it is what *you* need, not what others might imagine you need.

If you lack social support, look for ways to increase it. Perhaps you have met women/couples in a pregnancy exercise class or prenatal education class at your hospital or birthing center. Become active in community or religious organizations. Many such organizations are family-centered and will welcome your participation. Join a women's group. Spend more time with acquaintances from work or in your neighborhood. Renew old friendships. Strengthen your support system however you can, because you'll desperately need it as your baby grows.

Getting together with other parents who share similar concerns and needs has been shown to help prevent postpartum depression. Just seeing other moms struggling with the same problems you're grappling with can be validating. It's not that misery loves company, but rather that you may no longer feel as if something is wrong with you when you hear another human being voice your feelings, worries, complaints, and concerns.

There are additional benefits to knowing other parents with babies. You may learn about new ways of coping or resources for you and your child. You may be able to share something valuable you've here's also the possibility of babysitting trades. You may comfortable leaving your baby with a parent whom you've watched care for her own child rather than with a babysitter or in a daycare situation. By spending time with other moms, it's relatively easy to judge who sticks to the same standards as you do. Especially if you're nervous about leaving your baby with someone else, this may be the most comfortable way for both of you to begin. Besides that, it's affordable!

Aside from the benefits of babysitting and validation, socializing with other new parents means that you and your spouse can see how other couples deal with the stresses and strains of adjusting to parenthood. Seeing your own anxious bickering played out by others can give you an entirely new take on your problems. It can be a great relief as well to see that you're not the only couple who appears to be falling apart at the seams. Your partner may appreciate a chance to relate to other new parents and compare notes on why he can't get anything right, either.

Express and accept negative feelings, while also attending to positive feelings. It takes a great deal of emotional energy to avoid thinking about the hard part of this life change. The harder you work to push those scary or depressing feelings away, the less time and energy you have to live your life. If you can allow yourself to voice your negative feelings somewhere safe, you may find yourself free to experience the positive aspects of having a new baby as well. Writing your feelings out in a diary or journal, talking into a voice recorder, or expressing them to your partner, a family member, or trusted friend can help you cope, then move on. Again, meeting with other new parents may make it easier to do this, as those in the same boat will often understand more easily. Setting aside a time each day to feel and review your feelings can be helpful. You might need to set a timer to remind yourself to switch gears. After your "thinking time," do some deep breathing or stretching and make a list of your positive feelings.

Take breaks. How can you expect to fill up that pitcher again if you never get a few minutes off duty? Breaks are the law in the paid working world. In fact, in a forty hour work week composed of five eight-hour days, workers are entitled to two twenty minute breaks and a half hour lunch every day. Some approximation of this schedule of breaks should occur in your daily life as well. The new mother needs breaks alone, and the couple needs breaks from life as 'just parents.' This is a very important way to nurture your relationship with your partner and for each of you to nurture yourselves as individuals.

Try to learn to take time for yourself. Set aside a specified period during the week that is "your time," and devote it to doing whatever you want to do, without interruptions. You need a few minutes to read the paper, sip some tea, put your feet up and just dream. You also need an hour or two away to do something fun. You can practice taking as little as one half-hour to yourself two or three times a week. Developing a healthy respect for your needs for rest and relaxation—and teaching others in your life to respect these needs—may improve your postpartum adjustment and decrease your chances of postpartum problems.

Keep your expectations realistic. If you had grand ideas about reading the complete works of Shakespeare or wallpapering all the bedrooms while you were home on maternity leave, recognize these notions for what they are: completely unrealistic fantasies. The day-to-day care of a new baby is physically demanding and time-consuming to an incredible degree. If you get to shower every day, you're doing well.

Some women fall into the trap of expecting themselves to do everything in the same way they did before their baby arrived: keeping their homes spotless or fixing a three-course dinner most nights. You may be determined to return to work after six weeks' leave, no matter how you feel. Perhaps you expect yourself to listen to your friends' problems whenever they need a sympathetic ear or maybe you're accustomed to leading a fast-paced life, always on the go. If you expect your life to remain basically unchanged after you become a mother, your expectations are bound to shatter. Remember the title of this book: life will never be the same. Having a baby creates enormous physical, psychological, and interpersonal changes. Expect change. Be flexible in adapting to the many challenges of being a parent. The more you expect things to remain the same, the more likely you are to experience feelings of depression, anxiety, and loss.

Here are two things you can do to help you keep your expectations in line with reality. First of all, keep a list for a day or two of every baby care task you complete. Run a tally of the number of times you change the baby, feed the baby, wipe the spit up, wash the clothes, rock the baby, walk the baby, write a thank-you note, bathe the baby. At the end of a couple of days, you'll be amazed at how much you're accomplishing—even though these particular tasks might not have been exactly what you had in mind when you imagined life with baby. Nonetheless, all of these tasks are essential. Hiring a baby nurse to do them would cost a great deal of money. Secondly, if you must make a "to do" list beyond infant care, make it only two items long. If you accomplish one of these tasks, you're batting .500. Most professional baseball players would be thrilled with such a performance. Pat yourself on the back. You deserve it.

Practice lowering your expectations about being the perfect career woman, wife, or mother. Deliberately do less than what you think is adequate. See what response you get from yourself and others. Chances are no one will even notice. Check how cutting yourself some slack makes you feel. Practice doing less, or doing it imperfectly, on a weekly or daily basis. If you can't do this on your own, and you feel as if your expectations are controlling you, consult a professional therapist. Women who are able to give up unrelenting standards for themselves are less likely to develop a postpartum clinical condition.

Nurture your sense of humor. The ability to step back and see the absurdity and/or hilarity in a situation is always a valuable asset. This is especially critical when you have a new baby around. If you're having trouble seeing anything funny about your days, take a deep breath, sit back, and exhale slowly. Try to imagine looking back on this scene two or three or even ten years from now. Think about your funniest stories from other times in your life. Chances are they revolve around a minor disaster of one kind or another. Believe it or not, some of your worst days now will make great stories later on.

Judy, for example, had two babies in thirteen months, leaving her with full hands. The second baby was a real spit-up record setter, regurgitating after feedings so often that Judy became concerned and called the pediatrician. She was tired of needing to wear white every day and smelling like a cheese factory. The doctor asked her to tally how many times the baby spit up each day. She got to 147 before three p.m. one day—and then she gave up! While this drove her to tears at the time, it made a hilarious story by the time the baby turned one. (He was fine even in the midst of his spitting, gaining weight like crazy). Imagine what might seem funny about your own scenario three years from now. If you're having difficulty, check out some of Bill Cosby's or Robin Williams' comedy routines about parenthood from the video store. Look for the book *Sleeping Through the Night and Other Lies* by Sandi Kahn Shelton.

Besides trying to keep focused on the humor in your daily chaos, look for other ways to inject some levity into your life. Read the comics. Listen to comedy routines on radio or CD. Watch a funny TV program; YouTube rarely disappoints. Check out a joke book from the library or visit a favorite online humor site. Look at old childhood pictures or call up some old childhood friends. Assign your partner to bring home a joke or funny story. Figure out what works best to tickle your funny bone, then take five minutes each day to nurture your sense of humor. Your effort pays off in a better mood and an increased amount of energy.

Structure your day. In the evening, while you're still thinking clearly, sit down and plan out your agenda for the next day. It helps to have at least one outing to look forward to each day, even if it's just a walk around the block. If you feel anxious about going out, schedule a telephone call to a friend. Try to plan at least one event involving adult contact, beyond your partner's return in the evening. Plan for something fun, too, even something as simple as reading the comics or watching a TV show you enjoy. Such planning is an important way to regain a sense of control in your life, even if you're only controlling a few small events every day.

Postpone major life changes. The first several months postpartum are no time to decide anything that will have long-term consequences. If you are unhappy with your home, your job, your life, think change *within* rather than a complete revamping. Make your current residence more pleasing, or attend to what you like about your current job. While you won't be able to totally eliminate stress from your life in the postpartum period, there are still some elements you can control. Do not move, change jobs, file for divorce, or make any other big decisions unless you have absolutely no other choice. You'll be much better equipped to tackle such issues when your hormones are back in balance and you've begun to adjust to your new life as a mom. Partners are also advised to resist the urge to turn their lives any more upside-down than they are already. Sports car purchases, business start-ups, and triathlon training may need to wait.

When you put all these recommendations to work in your life, a little bit at a time, you are on your way to not only feeling great as a mom but preventing postpartum emotional problems. No one can do all of these things perfectly, or do them one hundred percent of the time. Try focusing on one for a few days until it begins to become a habit. Then add another. Taking charge in these few, but major, areas can work wonders for your stress levels. This is the basic foundation for your self-care plan: your key to motherhood survival.

3

Obstacles to Practicing Self-Care

The Short Version
(If You're Pressed for Time)

One of the most important things you can do to prevent or recover from postpartum emotional problems is to learn to take better care of yourself. As women, this is hard for us to do even when we aren't facing the physical and emotional demands of infant care. Unfortunately, most of us did not learn to practice self-care while growing up. We often feel like making our emotional health a priority will interfere with taking good care of our children, partners, families and friends. In fact, the exact opposite is true. The more you care for yourself, the more energy and peace of mind you will have and the less resentful and stressed you will feel. Take a few minutes now to think about the reasons you do not make your health and well-being a priority and decide what you can do to change this.

In this chapter, we explore the beliefs and habits that get in the way of taking care of yourself, emotionally or physically. Most of the time, these obstacles become clear if you can tune into the brain chatter, or self-talk, that bubbles up when you even think about taking time for you. This self-talk is just a habit. The best way to defeat these counterproductive beliefs is to repeat new phrases to yourself. This may seem silly or strange at first. You may doubt how this can work. Please try it for a few days before you judge its value for you.

The page number for each obstacle is listed below:

To survive your postpartum transition, and prevent the "normal crazy" from blossoming into a more serious episode of depression and anxiety, it may be helpful to explore these beliefs and habits. Once you are aware of these roadblocks, you can replace the negative ideas that get in the way of your ability to take care of yourself as best you can. Read the obstacles that seem to ring true for you in order to find concrete ideas about reprogramming those self-talk habits.

Exercise:
Two Minutes for Yourself

You may feel overwhelmed about the barriers to learning this new strategy of self-care. Find a quiet place, and close your eyes. Practice slow, deep breathing, so slow that your abdomen rises and falls. For two minutes, repeat to yourself with each exhaled breath: "Taking care of me benefits the baby." Pick the metaphor that works best for you. Picture that image in your head. When you take care of yourself, are you filling your pitcher, building your bank account, recharging your batteries? Each time thoughts weasel into your head, chastising you that something else is more important than taking time for you, take a deep breath and practice this image and the above phrase. Of course the baby must come first, but babies are good at making their needs known, and thus met. It's essential to care for yourself to be a good mom.

3

Obstacles To Practicing Self-Care

Historically in most cultures, women are the caretakers. From an early age, little girls feed, bathe, and clothe their baby dolls or stuffed animals. Think about your family as you were growing up: did Mom fix all the meals, do the dishes, fold the clothes, bathe the kids, and pick up the house while Dad plopped down in his easy chair and read the paper? Even if your parents divided the household responsibilities in a less traditional manner, most women becoming mothers today did not have a role model who took time for herself.

For many years, psychologists believed people reacted to stress by either fighting or fleeing, i.e., running away from a stressful situation. Research has shown that men and women respond differently when stressed. Women handle stress not by "fight or flee" but by "tend and befriend." When women are stressed, they often cope not by tending to their own needs, but by caring for their loved ones and socializing with other women. Hence, "tend and befriend" is the standard female model for managing stress. Just because this is the most *common* coping tool does not mean it is the most *productive*. Perhaps this strategy of tending to others when stressed is why women suffer depression twice as often as men do.

Think back to the analogy of the pitcher again. Certainly, caring for those you love and socializing with your friends may make you feel better at times. But if you always give and never take time to rejuvenate yourself, your ability to give to others, friends or family, will diminish. You'll wear yourself out. You can't give if your pitcher is empty and you are exhausted. Refer back to the self-care plan in chapter two for tips on how to avoid running on empty. You must take care of yourself, emotionally and physically, to be at your best.

However, if you are like most women, there are lots of mental obstacles to taking care of yourself. We call these obstacles to self-care. Obstacles to self-care are the deeply-conditioned expectations and rules about others' reactions if you choose to put yourself first. These are beliefs and concerns about how women, mothers in particular, must behave. Most of the time, these ideas lurk right beneath conscious awareness. You may not realize you believe these expectations and hold yourself to these standards of behavior until you suddenly face your own real-life baby doll to feed and clothe. Maybe you can keep these ideas at bay, living your independent life, until you begin to think of yourself as a mother. Then these considerable "shoulds" about what mothers do begin to sneak in, causing you to pause when you want to put yourself first.

The obstacles explored in this chapter are:

- Guilt — other demands are more important than my needs.
- My role is to take care of other people. It's what women do.
- Lack of time — I can't find the time to do the things I need to without adding this.
- I feel selfish when I do something for myself.
- I feel I don't deserve time for myself to do what I want.
- I'm afraid other people won't like me/will be angry with me.
- Never learned — My mother never did anything for herself, so why should I?
- Nice girls always put the other person first.
- Perfectionism — It takes all my time to do everything that needs to be done the "right" way.
- I think I can be healthy without doing this.

Along with an explanation of each obstacle are ideas on changing the underlying thoughts. If an obstacle represents something you say to yourself when faced with a choice of "do for me" versus "do for another," we offer some new words to repeat to yourself to combat the guilt, anxiety, and blame that keep you making choices that may exhaust you. You need not read the whole list in depth. If only two of the obstacles listed ring true for you, skip to those sections and read just those two. Then, practice the new thoughts suggested in those sections.

Sometimes, women say that these obstacles show up as running dialogue, thoughts that are chastising, critical, parental. In other cases, women report that the obstacles are images, not words. Instead of hearing any of the negative phrases we've listed here in your head, you have flashes of a disapproving face or of your mother tidying the kitchen while everyone else watched a favorite show on TV. If you are a pictures person, you may need to transfer what we suggest here from words to images. Imagine others in your life showing approval, or see yourself relaxed and more effective as a mom because you've taken time for you. Repetition of new phrases (and/or concentrating on new images) will seem strange and even useless at first. It's hard to see how changing the words or pictures in your head can make a difference. Trust us, it does. Repetition like this is how you learn anything, from times tables to French to a tennis stroke. Give yourself a week, know you won't believe the new talk (or image) right away, and watch what happens. Again and again, women return to our offices and say, "I didn't really think this would work—and was I surprised!"

Of course, when you have a new baby, and throughout your life as a mother, there are practical considerations of time and energy that influence your ability to practice self-care, too. Your children, being children, usually must come first. They cannot do for themselves in the way that adults can. You want to take good care of them. But the two sets of needs, yours and theirs, are not mutually exclusive. Your needs are just as important, even while often deferred. There is a balance between your needs and those of your loved ones. By tackling the underlying challenges to self-care, you will feel better and will be more able to care for those you love.

Obstacles to Self-Care

Guilt: Other demands are more important.

How can I take time for me when there are bottles to be made? Diapers to be changed? Bills to be paid? Deadlines to meet at work? My partner works all day too and deserves a chance to unwind at the end of the day. Every day, as a woman and a mother, there are millions of competing tasks. Managing a household and caring for children are endless tasks, whether you leave them for forty hours to attend to other work or not. These are important demands.

Despite the importance of the many tasks facing you each day, you must make choices. You must prioritize. Which tasks are really critical? Can the tub get cleaned every two weeks instead of every week? Are fresh-cut and steamed vegetables really more critical to health than the frozen ones you cook in half the time? Are you truly the only one who can pay the bills? Can your assistant at work make some of these phone calls? Share the responsibilities as much as possible, hire out or barter for what you can, ask for and accept help from those who care about you, or maybe from those who owe you favors.

Guilt is a choice. When you feel guilty, you are saying that some activity is more important than your well-being. Choose to raise your needs to the level of your child's needs, or at least to second place rather than not even on the list. Choose to affirm, "I am worth it." Do not feel guilty about being a human who needs rest and relaxation. Often by simply trying to choose your self-care over some less essential household task one time, you will see results. You will see that you are better able to smile at your baby when you take half an hour of her nap to read a book you enjoy. Recite, "I choose to make my care a priority – and there is payoff for my baby." Say, "I am more important than whether the house is spotless."

Caretaking is my role as a woman.

Traditionally, women are the caregivers in most societies. This custom dates to the days when people were hunters and gatherers. Children were breastfed for long periods of time and often strapped to their mothers' backs for the first year or longer. Great danger existed if the baby was off mama's back; a passing saber tooth tiger might decide baby would make a great snack. Mom did not do too well tracking that mastodon with baby weighing her down, either. Biologically, women needed to be the constant nurturers, while men brought home the food for survival.

Enter the twenty-first century. Industrialization, birth control pills, and the women's movement and subsequent entry into the work force have all moved us in the direction of two highly involved parents. With this historical perspective, it has become clear that the division of labor in which the female tends to all things family while the male deals with the outside world is outdated. Certainly, when a mother is breastfeeding, the father cannot be as involved in the feeding of the baby. Biologically, that is where the division of labor by male/female lines ends. Plenty of baby care chores revolve around needs other than feeding. Psychologists know that men are just as capable of childcare as are women. Not only are men capable, but they are doing more and more with their children. This benefits everyone. Children get different needs met through interaction with father than with mother. They develop different skills. Girls become more achievement oriented when their dads are active parents. Boys become more compassionate and caring. Fathers become closer to their children. Moms get more breaks.

Sharing the childcare tasks benefits everyone in the family. Even if you choose to be the primary caretaker, this still does not require total self-sacrifice because of your biology. Your needs are still important. Recite, "My needs are important too." Say, "Kids need both parents involved in the day to day tasks." Repeat, "Dads can be as loving as moms." If you are a single mom, relying on relatives to share the childcare tasks is equally important. Say, "The baby learns to trust others when I let my sister care for him."

Lack of time for self-care.

Children are demanding. They make their needs known. Messy houses seem to scream, too: "Load these dishes" or "Make that bed." Bosses inflict deadlines. Friends and family members require attendance at the birthday party, the golf game, the hospital bedside. Everyone in your life has needs. Others may seem better at demanding those needs are met than you are. Your needs sink to the bottom of the 'to do' list. There simply seems to be no time.

No one will make time for you but you. No one will take care of you but you. No one is a mind reader, so your mother or your partner or your best friend does not realize you are running on empty unless you speak up. These are all hard truths about being an adult and especially about being a parent. You have to make time. You and only you. Again, this means making choices. Choose to put yourself first — at least once each day.

Another part of making time for yourself happen is adjusting your expectations about how much time is needed. Ideally, you desire a forty minute soak in the tub, followed by an hour lounging in bed with that trashy novel. Think in smaller terms. Take five minutes out of each hour to practice deep breathing or to perform some crunches.

Or take twenty minutes to disappear for a rest in the bedroom when your partner comes home. Think in terms of multi-tasking, too. Walk the baby in the stroller. Lie on the floor with a magazine, next to the baby while he has his "tummy time," and smile at him occasionally. Repeat to yourself, "Time for me is essential," "I can take five minutes every other hour for me" — or at least twenty minutes once a day!

I feel selfish.

Many women are taught to think of others, to *always* put others' needs first. This is often presented in a very black or white fashion. Either you put others' needs first *all the time*, or you are selfish. There is little perspective on the middle ground, that you can be a considerate person and still put yourself first every now and then. Selfish people always put themselves first, every waking minute. People who practice self-care can maintain a balance, tending to the feelings or needs of those around them without totally denying their own need for rest, relaxation, nourishment, and fun. Self-care means self-preservation, not selfishness. It is what allows us to thrive in our lives, not merely survive.

Talk positively to yourself when you have managed to steal away for some activity you enjoy. Label what you are doing as self-preservation. You are not selfish. You are working to find the balance between your needs and the needs of others. Recount in your head the many giving things you have done today and tell yourself you have earned this brief respite from the needs of others. Repeat, "It's self-preservation, not selfishness."

I don't deserve it.

You may feel that resources have become extremely valuable once your baby is born. Time is at a premium; extra cash may be hard to find. Certainly you want to give the best to your baby. Women may devalue their own needs, believing the myth of "only a mother." You are only a mother — how hard can that be? Why would you need breaks when all you have done today is sit on the couch feeding a baby? Your partner is working a "real" job — certainly breaks are more deserved after battling customers all day. You may devalue what you do in terms of spending money, too. Why would you need to order take out food for dinner when you have not done anything today? An attitude like this devalues the hard work that you are doing.

Falling into the trap of denying your needs because you don't deserve it is often related to issues of self-worth, as well as issues of the value or difficulty of the job you are doing. Pay attention to what you are saying in your head. You may feel like less of a person now if you are only a mommy. Even if you are working outside the home, you may feel your brain has fled, and you are contributing no longer to your employer's mission. Tune in to how you are belittling your skills, your efforts and your time with your baby by repeating such negatives.

You are the most important person to your baby. No one can be a mother to your baby but you. You, and only you, are the mother your baby needs. As we have said before, you will be a better mother if you take care of yourself emotionally and physically. And if your baby deserves the best mother possible (of course!), then you have to take care of your needs. If your baby's mother does not deserve it, who does? Practice reciting to yourself, "My baby deserves the best—and that means me!" "To be the best for my baby, I deserve to take care of me." "Parenting is one of the most important jobs I'll ever do, and with all I do, I've earned time for me."

I am afraid others will be angry/I am afraid others won't like me.

Underlying this obstacle to change is another example of cultural conditioning. Little girls are often taught to attend to other's feelings. "Why is Joelle crying?" a mother asks. "Did you make your friend mad?" she scolds. The implied message is that you can make a person feel a certain way, and that if you make someone feel badly, you are doing something wrong. Girls are charged with "being nice" and seeing to it that others feel good. Since many women are raised with the idea that they are responsible for how others feel, they fear the emotional reactions of their friends, loved ones, and even complete strangers. Not only do women believe they have control over the feelings of others, they often learn that their own feelings are less important than others' feelings.

The truth is that everyone is responsible for their own feelings and only their own feelings. Most of the time, you cannot *make* another person mad. You do not set out to purposely anger another person. That other person reacts in an angry way, often to our complete surprise. Likewise, you may recognize times when a friend is sad, and you can not *make* her happy. You can support her, and listen, and even do nice things for her, but the decision to feel better is really her own. No one can make another person feel any certain emotion—the responsibility for our feelings lies totally within us, and only us. If practicing self-care *makes* someone angry at you, that is really his/her issue. You still have to take care of yourself, regardless of how others react. Would you forgo vaccinations for your child, given that you believe in their essential value, if it would make your anti-vaccination mother-in-law angry? You know that you must make your own decisions about what is best for your family. That includes self-care.

Another facet of this obstacle is the idea that anger is scary. Anger is just a feeling. When people who matter are angry with you, it usually passes. So try on the 'so what?' mentality. *So what* if leaving the baby in the gym nursery three times weekly so you can exercise to feel better makes your mother mad? Is the baby well-cared for? Then is it really anyone's business but your own? So what! Repeat, "So what—those feelings aren't my responsibility" or, "So what—I know I am a better mom because of it" or "So what—I can't help it that my mom is angry that I am learning to take care of myself when she never did."

Much of our value as women comes from approval by others. Do you feel like a good person because you are liked? When others disapprove, you may feel like a lesser being. This is another good time to practice the 'so what' mentality. If someone disapproves of the way in which you take care of yourself in an effort to be a better parent, is that really important? Remember, you are the expert on you. You know what is best for you, your baby, and your family. So what if your neighbor or mother does not agree with what you are doing? Repeat, "I am the expert on me." "I know what is best for me and my baby." You have survived being disliked before, have you not? You will survive it again. It is a valuable skill to learn.

I never learned how to take care of myself.

Your mother never sat down until all the work was finished at night. Your favorite aunt keeps her house spotless, and she last went to the movies with a girlfriend in 1962. Models of effective self-care are scarce; most women subscribe to one or more of the beliefs described here as obstacles to self-care. You never learned; you really are clueless about how to make time, or even what to do with it when you have it. So you wander the grocery store when your mother comes to give you a break. That's a chore, even an enjoyable one for some. You need a more renewing kind of fun. Time to learn to take care of yourself.

Learning to take care of yourself begins with the assurance, as stated above, that this is a good thing. Recite, "I will be a better mommy if I have some fun." Then begin to explore what might be fun or relaxing. What have you always wanted to do? To learn? Give yourself a couple of months to experiment. Take a class. Try a craft. Pick up a different kind of book or puzzle. Practice a yoga pose five minutes each day. Talk to other mothers about how they unwind. Remember what you did as a girl or young woman that brought joy and try that. It takes work, but it begins with permission, then experimentation, followed by persistence. Many women find that they are so depleted that it takes several weeks before they begin to feel less overwhelmed. Say, "I can keep at this until I find something that works for me!"

Nice girls always put others first.

It is an admirable quality to consider the needs of others. Putting others first is something to strive for in many instances, and this goal will certainly make you a good mother. As we have said, children's needs must come first, and that goes beyond 'nice' to essential. Balance is as important here as in any part of life. If you always strive for 'nice,' putting others first, you may find yourself last on the list. No one will take care of your needs but you. If you aren't attuned to meeting your own needs, it becomes harder and harder to be 'nice.' Instead of smiling at others and feeling calm and giving, you end up feeling snappy and irritable because everyone gets what they need but you.

Forget the absolutes. Toss out the idea that if you are not putting others first *all the time*, then you are no longer nice. It is not black and white. Beware of the absolutes that make you feel awful: words like 'always,' 'never.' You can still be a considerate person to your loved ones and meet your own needs too. Review what was said in the '**I am afraid others will be angry**' section about attending to other's feelings and opinions too much. Encourage yourself by repeating, "I can put my own needs first sometimes and still be nice to others." Say, "Nice girls need to be nice to themselves, too."

Perfectionism: All my time is needed to do it "right."

Striving for everything to be right, especially *right all the time* is a huge obstacle to taking care of yourself, whether you have a new baby or not. Perfection is a myth. No one can achieve making everything right, chores completed, all in order, one hundred percent of the time. New mothers, used to having everything neat, tidy, arranged, and on time, frequently exhaust themselves when they continue this already unrealistic standard into the postpartum period. Don't add this Type A form of crazy to the normal crazy of the postpartum period. You are human. You have a whole new person to care for, manage, and soothe. If you don't abandon the perfectionism goal, all your time will be eaten up in doing things "right," and you will be exhausted. Suddenly, your child will be three and you will have missed all those magic moments because you jumped up to load the dishes, wrote literary quality thank you notes, and organized the pantry. This new phase of life calls for a new standard.

Try this new standard: instead of perfection, you are striving for perfectly good. Perfectly good is not perfect, but it is attainable and acceptable. Perfectly good means whatever you can accomplish is working, manageable. Perfectly good ranges from "good enough" to "excellent." If friends stop by, and there are dishes in the sink, take five minutes to pick up the newspapers in the living room and ignore the dishes. That is perfectly good. If you are five minutes late to the pediatrician, that is perfectly good. The pediatrician will still keep you waiting twenty minutes and not even know if you were a few minutes late. If your baby's blue shirt is a slight shade off from those blue socks, that is perfectly good. Perspective is the key. Will whatever you are striving to make perfect really matter in thirty minutes, or three years? Will your child remember playing cars on the floor with mom, or the fact that the floor was always vacuumed and toy free? Will your child remember a relaxed, attentive mom, or a mom stressed by trying to be perfect?

Your thinking is really a matter of talking to yourself. Psychologists call this "self-talk." What you say to yourself influences the way you feel. Given this link between the words in your head and your emotions, new self-talk about perfection is critical. Try repeating, "Perfect is not possible—but I can get to perfectly good." Say, "Nobody's perfect—and my baby loves me anyway." Recite, "Taking ten minutes for me right now is more important than getting all the clothes out of the dryer." Tell yourself, "It is more important for my baby that I give lots of hugs and kisses than that I am perfect." For more on this topic, consult Dr. Dunnewold's book *Even June Cleaver Would Forget the Juice Box: Cut Yourself Some Slack (and Still Raise Great Kids) in the Age of Extreme Parenting.*

I can be healthy without doing this.

For all your adult life, you have managed just fine. You have achieved, you have excelled, you have avoided health problems. How is now any different? Why should you have to begin to worry about vitamins, rest, exercise, or fitting in the fun? Your life has always rocked along just fine.

The answer may lie in what psychologists call the mind-body connection. The mind-body connection indicates that your mind and your body interact in inseparable ways. If you are feeling sick, you often become lethargic and depressed. If you are depressed and anxious, your immune system will function less effectively. Cause and effect move back and forth in both directions: your emotional state can make you physically sick, just as your physical well-being can affect your mood. This leads to the concept of "wellness" as the harmony of the mind and body. In other words, the brain and body are functioning as one. When one of the two is not working properly due to lack of sleep, sickness, or stress, then you are not considered "well." The connection between the mind and body is powerful, and research has shown that emotional self-care contributes directly to physical health. One study observed medical residents. Doctors in training typically work several days around the clock, and then are off for a day or two. Taking care of others at all hours of the day and night is certainly a physical stress, much like having a newborn baby. The residents were divided into two groups. One group wrote in a journal over the course of their week, jotting down thoughts and feelings. The control group did not. When blood samples were drawn, the residents who had done the journaling showed increased immune system function, meaning the journaling group got sick less often. The control group of residents seemed to catch every germ that walked into the hospital, missing many more days of work from illness.

From pregnancy on, your mind and body encounter significant stresses, due to hormone changes and lifestyle changes. Research with new mothers has indicated that it can take up to a year after birth for the state of your immune system to return to normal function. In that time, your wellness may be sacrificed if you do not attend to your physical and emotional needs. Another way to think about this may be to envision an old-fashioned scale, or balance. Scales like this have two pans suspended from a crossbar. If in one pan you place all the emotional changes and increased physical demands that parenthood brings, that pan will sink to the table. Now, imagine placing the strategies for self-care and coping into the other pan. Perhaps you add exercise to the coping pan; the pan of change rises a bit. Now add some fun, in ten minute doses, and maybe the pan will rise again. Add a healthy diet and vitamins, and the coping pan may level out with the pan that holds all the changes.

Perhaps you can sail through this transition in your life without major changes in your pattern of self-care. But why take the chance? If self-care will make you less irritable, less anxious, and less likely to catch each virus that comes along, don't you owe that to yourself and your baby? Make your mantra, "Taking care of me is important too" and "Self-care makes me a better mother." Self-care may have been dispensable before you were a mom, but now that the demands are greater, it is essential.

Steps to Further Change

Confronting the obstacles to change in your own head and habits is essential for effective use of a self-care plan as described in chapter two. If you find that the suggestions here and in chapter two leave you wishing for more help with these issues, be sure to read chapter six, where there are sections on negative thinking and combating perfectionism.

4

The Spectrum of Postpartum Emotions

Normal Crazy: The Blues and Normal Postpartum Adjustment

The Short Version
(If You're Pressed for Time)

Even though you may have felt well-prepared for motherhood, some of your reactions may come as a surprise. In this chapter, we describe the normal range of emotions that women often go through after the birth of a baby. You already know about the anticipation, joy, and delight a baby can bring. We present the rest of the story here.

Because childbirth is a major life change, it's natural for you to have some negative feelings about it. Until you have time to read the in-depth description and examples, here's the short course in normal postpartum reactions.

The Blues. This is the term used to describe the prevalent tearfulness, fatigue, insomnia, exhaustion, and irritability of the first two to three days after the birth of a baby. Striking fifty to eighty percent of all new mothers, the blues are very common. Feelings associated with the blues usually go away within a week or two and tend to be only slightly bothersome to the new mother. However, pay attention to the severity of the blues that you experience. The blues used to be considered harmless because these feelings would resolve on their own. Research now shows that women who have a very difficult time emotionally in the seventy-two hours after birth may be at increased risk of developing true postpartum depression and anxiety in the period two to three months postpartum.

Normal Adjustment. The next level of distress felt by new mothers is categorized as "normal adjustment." "Normal crazy" might be a more accurate description. You may have many of the feelings of the blues, plus anxiety, mood swings, and anger. These feelings are completely normal, but feel crazy because of societal expectations that this is a wonderful time in your life. In fact, these negative feelings of the normal adjustment period make perfect sense. New mothers are sleep-deprived, exhausted, and typically overwhelmed. They're thrown into a new job for which there's no adequate training available and are given sole responsibility for a completely vulnerable and complex human being who arrives in the world with no instruction manual. The mother's negative feelings may continue for up to two months, and usually are "on again, off again" in nature, with many good days mixed in with the bad.

This chapter describes "the blues" and normal adjustment on the spectrum of postpartum emotions.

Exercise:
Two Minutes for Yourself

You may find yourself becoming extremely self-critical, telling yourself such things as: "You are so stupid! What's wrong with you? Can you even take care of your baby? You wanted this baby so badly and now all you can do is worry; get it together! What kind of a person are you to wish your old life back? What a lousy mother you are!"

Acknowledge what you are telling yourself. Imagine instead that you are talking to a child or a close friend who is tormenting herself in this way. What can you tell her to make her feel better? How can you encourage her, and recognize all the hard work she's done so far?

Close your eyes, take four deep breaths, then say to yourself, "You are strong and competent, and this is really hard work. Just hang in there."

4

The Spectrum of Postpartum Emotions

Normal Crazy: The Blues and Normal Postpartum Adjustment

Facing any major life change, whether marriage, a new job, or a move to a new home, involves a range of feelings. As a culture, we expect such adjustments to be filled with emotions from exaltation to harried irritability. This is also true for the transition to parenthood. While the picture painted by society includes a smiling mother and cooing baby, there is growing acceptance that becoming a parent involves stress, resulting in negative and positive feelings as we adjust to this new role. There is no one way that all new mothers and fathers feel. Some parents breeze right through, without a care, while others have quite pressing worries. As health professionals have studied the range of emotions individuals feel after the birth of a baby, they have conceptualized these clinical conditions as a range or continuum of reactions, not discrete experiences. In the original version of this book, *Postpartum Survival Guide,* we first published the idea of this continuum as a spectrum of postpartum emotions. This continuum includes not only the normal postpartum responses, but the more difficult clinical conditions. In this chapter, we will focus on the baby blues, postpartum exhaustion, and normal adjustment experienced by most new moms. Chapter eight details the more reactive end of the spectrum, looking in depth at postpartum depression, anxiety, and psychosis.

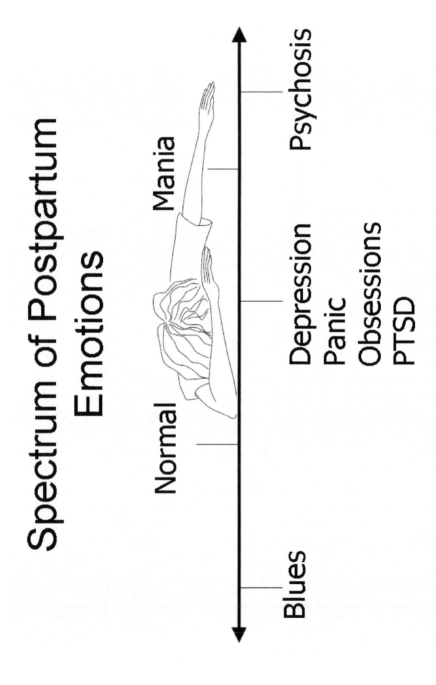

Spectrum of Postpartum Emotions

Blues

Normal

Mania

Depression
Panic
Obsessions
PTSD

Psychosis

The majority of new mothers undergo biological, social, and psychological changes that do not interfere with their day-to-day functioning and are considered to be part of the normal adjustment to having a child.

The Baby Blues

As many as eighty percent of women go through the baby blues. The blues are a mild change in mood which occurs twenty-four to forty-eight hours postpartum, likely because of the dramatic hormonal changes brought about by pregnancy, labor and childbirth. Women with the blues report crying easily, reacting with irritation over trivialities they'd normally ignore, suffering fatigue, having difficulty sleeping, being more emotional than usual, or feeling slight anxiety or agitation. For most women, the baby blues do not last beyond two weeks, although some women may have mild symptoms for up to six weeks following birth.

Most of the time, the blues resolve without intervention, as women get more rest and hormones begin to even out. In most cases, the blues are not worth any worry. Some women have extreme blues, however. Research suggests that the severity of the blues predicts postpartum adjustment between six and ten weeks after the birth. If you have a really tough time emotionally in the first week after your baby's birth, put a note on your calendar to "check-in" emotionally in eight to ten weeks. You may wish to follow-up, just as a preventive measure, with a mental health professional some time in the second month of your baby's life.

A Real Mom's Story: The Baby Blues

Regina and Tom fought fertility problems for seven years before finally conceiving twins. Both ecstatic, they breezed through the pregnancy with only momentary dips into terror as they contemplated handling TWO babies. Luckily, both Regina and Tom came from large families. She had five sisters; he had seven siblings. All this extended family lived nearby, with no shortage of grandmothers, aunts, uncles, and nieces clamoring for baby assistance duty. Regina spent two weeks on bed rest at the end of the pregnancy, giving her cabin fever. She was irritable and tearful at times, feeling battered from within by the babies' constant kicking and poking. Tom coached her through cheerily. He made posters with copies of the sonogram pictures, writing encouraging statements such as "Here are our babies!" "Any time now!" and "Good job Mom." He mounted these posters all around their bedroom, so Regina could see the results of her efforts everywhere she turned. A planned Cesarean section at thirty-eight weeks produced two healthy boys.

The excitement and plummeting hormones overwhelmed Regina completely. She spent most of the first days in the hospital in tears: tears of joy alternating with tears of fear. How could she handle two babies? She had so wanted a girl. What was she going to do with boys, after growing up in a family of girls? She knew nothing about boys!

All those family members traipsed through the hospital room, oohing and ahhing over the twins. Regina cried again. How could everyone else seem so in love with these babies? All she felt was terror. One of Regina's sisters was a La Leche League leader who stayed with Regina for a whole day, helping her smoothly initiate the babies to the breast. Both babies eagerly took to nursing, giving small sighs as the colostrum dribbled from their sleepy mouths. As she gazed at them, it slowly dawned on Regina: they were just babies. It did not matter if they were boys or girls; these were the babies she had been craving for so long. She breathed a tentative sigh of relief.

Over the first week at home, Regina had a few more tearful and terrified moments. With all that eager family help, she always had someone to hold the babies. She napped when the babies napped and often even when they didn't, since there was always a willing relative to give her a break. By the end of the second week, the whole family had begun to settle into a rhythm. Sitting on the couch with her head on Tom's shoulder, each parent cradling a sleeping baby, Regina relaxed fully at last. She might cry every now and then, but this was it—they would be okay.

Checklist of Symptoms for The Blues:

- o   Crying
- o   Irritability
- o   Anger
- o   Insomnia
- o   Exhaustion
- o   Tension

- o   Anxiety
- o   Restlessness
- o   Emotionality

Normal Adjustment and Postpartum Exhaustion

What psychologists consider normal postpartum adjustment involves an extension of the symptoms of the blues through the first two months after birth. In other words, if you are past the time frame for the blues, but still have many negative feelings, you've probably moved along the continuum into the normal adjustment category.

Normal adjustment is a misleading term, because this new life does not feel *normal*. Angela McBride, in her book *The Growth and Development of Mothers*, suggests that a better term would be "normal crazy." Most new mothers have mixed positive and negative feelings and thoughts, but society leads us to believe that such reactions are somehow abnormal. In support of this view, the popular media portray new mothers as happy, loving, confident, and calm. This picture omits any negative reactions to the hard job of managing a new baby.

We believe that all new mothers experience some degree of "normal craziness" as they adjust to their new infants. The amount of difficulty a woman encounters depends on a host of biological, psychological, and social factors, as well as the type of baby she has (some babies are much easier to deal with than others). These factors vary from woman to woman as well as for the same woman at different times in her life. It is rare for any woman to breeze through the physical adjustments and hard work of feeding, changing, and comforting a baby twenty-four hours a day, all while trying to restore her control over her own body. Most new mothers encounter periods of fatigue, depression, irritability, worry, tearfulness, and doubts about their attractiveness and parenting skills. Mild sleeping problems, appetite changes, and a complete loss of sexual interest are also common.

Honey Watts, M.A., RSW, of Calgary, Canada has suggested that postpartum exhaustion may be a distinct category along this adjustment portion of the continuum. In postpartum exhaustion, women feel fairly well psychologically; they feel neither depressed nor anxious. However, a woman with postpartum exhaustion may feel overwhelmed and "bone-tired," simply unable to function. She may not be sleeping well during the day or night. Instead of resting, she is busy meeting the needs of her baby, the household, and other family members. Mothers in this category may report numerous physical symptoms such as headaches or stomach problems. In the pattern of postpartum exhaustion, many of these symptoms disappear when the baby begins to follow a regular schedule. As the baby starts to nap at regular times, and to sleep six or seven hours through the night, the mother can recover from sleep deprivation. This process can take several weeks, but then the new mother feels like herself again.

A Real Mom's Story: Postpartum Exhaustion

Maria was a single parent, having reached her late thirties with no suitable marriage partner in sight. She had always wanted to be a mother, so she chose artificial insemination as her path to this important life goal. Maria had a full support system, with two sisters and several close friends nearby who promised to support her in this daunting task of single parenting. The pregnancy went smoothly, and before Maria knew it she was home with tiny Darby, a seven pound three ounce wonder. Maria had saved money and worked hard at her accounting office and felt that the short term disability, accumulated sick leave and vacation, and savings would carry her through an adequate maternity leave. She enrolled Darby in an on-site day care facility even before she was born, knowing that having this settled was essential to her own well-being after the birth. For the first three days at home, all went well. Maria and Darby slept around the clock, Maria waking only to feed herself or the baby. Her sisters and friends took turns bringing meals, so Maria had only to wake up, stick something in the microwave, eat it, and lie down again with the baby. Before Maria knew what had hit her, the baby was two weeks old and working into a more definite pattern of sleep and wakefulness. It seemed neither of them had been dressed since returning from the hospital.

Always one to take charge, Maria decided they needed more structure. She set up a plan for herself, tackling a bit of housework, thank you notes, or an errand each day, instead of napping when the baby napped. But the baby was still eating every two hours, and Maria was having difficulty going back to sleep at night, often tossing and turning until Darby's next feeding. Sleep deprivation was catching up with her. "I am so tired" was the limit of her conversation when her support system called every day to check on her. "My back hurts; my hip hurts; I feel as if I have run a marathon." Maria felt so pulled—she wanted her house to be tidy, but she was *so* tired. Her sisters compared notes and decided they needed to intervene, setting up a schedule of relief. Someone would straighten up the house or throw in a load of laundry, someone else would run to the grocery, and a third friend would hold the baby in the afternoon so Maria might nap. Against Maria's protests that "I can do this on my own—I am only tired," her sisters and friends persisted for several weeks. Darby began to sleep for longer periods of time, both in the daytime and at night. That first six hour stretch at night unnerved Maria. She woke three times, catching her breath in a silent scream, wondering when the baby would wake up. With additional six hour stretches on consecutive nights, Maria caught up on her sleep. She was able to tackle some of the household responsibilities on her own. As the end of her maternity leave approached, Maria began taking Darby to the day care for small bits of time each day, leaving the baby while she caught up a bit on sleep and on chores. When she returned to work, Maria was not completely rested, but she was no longer so exhausted that she could not think straight.

Checklist of Symptoms for Postpartum Exhaustion

o   Denial of depression or anxiety
o   Feeling overwhelmed
o   Inability to sleep or rest
o   Physical symptoms (headaches, stomachaches)

"Normal Crazy": Normal Postpartum Adjustment

Many normal adjustment problems are caused by the hormonal changes that accompany pregnancy and childbirth. The enormous psychosocial transition of new motherhood must also be taken into account. When a woman has a new baby, particularly her first, she begins to reevaluate all her ideas about who she is. She may now compare herself, favorably or not, to her mother. She may have very distinct ideas about the kind of parent she wishes to be. She may wonder how she will bring her former childless self together with this new person who is suddenly a parent. If the new mother is changing her work status to care for the baby, these changes will be amplified.

Partners may face similar adjustments in self-image. New fathers must often deal with increased worries about financial needs and responsibilities. The demands on their time may mean that cherished leisure activities have to go out the window. New fathers may be faced with a partner who doesn't look or act at all like the person they married. In addition, they're expected to be involved with childcare responsibilities, even though many men have no model to follow in this area, as their own fathers were more than likely uninvolved with their infants.

The couple must also negotiate the mine field of their changed and changing relationship and household responsibilities. It's hard to make plans in advance when the baby's personality and the mother's condition after childbirth are big unknowns. All the ground rules for a household and a relationship change when a baby arrives. It's rare for a couple to simply *know* the right adjustments to make to find their sense of balance again. Trial and error is inevitable in negotiating these questions for practically every couple.

New parents often need to reevaluate their relationship with the family in which they were raised. Becoming a parent may allow you a greater sense of adulthood and freedom from your family of origin. Alternatively, it may tighten bonds that have relaxed with time and distance. What must you do to graduate to the world of grown-ups in your family? Seeing yourself as an adult does not guarantee other family members will see you that way.

With all these changes and negotiations going on, it's no wonder that the period following the birth of a baby is stressful. This is true whether the baby is the first or the fifth. With each child, the tasks, time demands, and alliances in the family shift. As with any stressful life stage, symptoms and negative feelings easily appear. "Normal crazy" is usually not a problem. Most parents face it, and, with the support of family and friends, eventually regain some balance in their lives.

A Real Mom's Story: Normal Postpartum Adjustment

Liz was an associate in a high-powered New York law firm. Shortly before she was due to make partner, at the age of forty-one, she became pregnant. Both she and her husband were astonished, as

Liz had never been pregnant before and always assumed she was unable to conceive. Her husband, also a lawyer, agreed with her that they could give parenthood a try, but he made Liz promise him that she wouldn't let having a baby ruin her career. Their marriage had always been based on shared professional values and an attachment to the upscale lifestyle provided by their dual income.

Even though Liz received a lot of ribbing at work for "getting knocked up," the firm granted her an eight-week paid maternity leave. She continued working into her ninth month, and made it clear that she wanted nothing to do with a "mommy track" job. She still intended to make partner.

Then David was born. Liz fell in love with her baby more than she could ever have imagined. As her precious eight weeks at home with him began to whiz by, Liz became increasingly frantic. She kept telling herself that every moment with David had to count; she felt secretly worried that he wouldn't bond with her in their short time together.

David was a placid baby and a good sleeper. At the end of three weeks, Liz found herself waking him up in the middle of the night so she could nurse him and gaze into his eyes. She and her husband had gone to great pains to find a terrific professional nanny with impeccable references, but Liz tossed and turned at night worrying that they'd somehow made a bad choice. No one could love and care for her baby the way she did. She fantasized about handing in her resignation at work. Her mind even wandered to taking David and leaving her husband.

During the final two weeks, the nanny came to their apartment every day so David could learn to take a bottle from her. Liz was supposed to spend this time resting or doing nice things for herself, but instead she locked herself in the bathroom and cried. How could she even contemplate returning to the cutthroat culture of the law firm with her leaking breasts and her sudden tendency to break into tears for no reason? How could she contemplate leaving David at home with the nanny? Liz's husband just shook his head when he came home one night and found her bedraggled, stained with breast milk and spit-up, crying her eyes out. "Must be hormones," he said to her. "This just isn't like you at all. Remember, Lizzy? You're the one who makes other people cry!" Liz wanly nodded her head, making an effort to look cheerful for him.

During the seventh week, Liz switched moods like a changing traffic light. She sat for an hour, reveling in her baby's sweet gaze, rocking him as he cooed, feeling incredibly content. She wanted to soak up every tiny ounce of him, storing the feeling, smell, and sight of him to carry her through her return to work. Then she handed him to the nanny and ran from the room sobbing. Liz's husband brought her a new briefcase one evening to commemorate her upcoming return to work. She was delighted at first, then ended up raging at him for reminding her that her leave was ending. When the nanny gently suggested the next day that Liz might want to check in with her doctor before she returned to her job, Liz became furious at her, too, and then dissolved in tears. "I can't do this!" she wailed, relieved finally to be admitting the truth to someone. "I'm not even myself anymore. I don't know who I am! I used to be a very, very formidable attorney. Everyone was afraid of me."

"Of course they were," said the nanny, patting Liz's hand. "And they will be yet, as soon as your body settles down and finds its balance again. The best thing you can do for you and David is get some sleep."

With help and encouragement from the nanny, a very kind person, Liz managed to get herself together enough to make a decent impression when she returned to work. But she knew that becoming a mother had changed her forever. She still planned to make partner, but that long-sought goal had lost much of its meaning for her. She had a frank talk with her husband, letting him know that her values had really changed. Once she got her promotion, she planned to take a leave until David was ready for preschool. She had her whole life to be a highly paid attorney but David would be a baby for only a very short time.

Checklist of Symptoms for Normal Postpartum Adjustment

o   Crying, tearfulness
o   Irritability
o   Anger
o   Sleep disturbance
o   Fatigue
o   Dysphoria (negative mood)
o   Appetite changes

o   Loss of interest in usual activities
o   Anxiety
o   Mood swings
o   Feelings of doubt (re: attractiveness, parenting skills, etc.)

The Role of Emotional Adjustment

Remember, emotional ups and downs are just part of everyone's adjustment to parenthood. If you did not have these new challenges, you would have less of a chance to grow into this new role. Try to accept that this emotional upheaval is only natural and expected. You are not defective for having these struggles. You are just a new mom, facing one of the hardest jobs and most challenging changes you will ever conquer. Becoming a parent is a learning process and it takes time to develop confidence.

Things become more difficult if the new mother obsesses about what these reactions mean about her as a person. If she thinks her unhappiness or doubts reveal her to be a "bad," "sick," or less-than-perfect person, she may feel guilty. If she (or family members) question her mental health, parenting ability, or achievement of a bond with her baby, finding her balance again may be much more daunting. When these difficulties continue to affect her ability to complete daily tasks or worsen over a two-to-five week period, a red flag goes up for a postpartum clinical condition.

This represents another step along the continuum of postpartum emotions. Look at the spectrum again on page 48. If your baby is only one or two weeks old, your symptoms most likely fall into the category of the blues. If your baby is older than three weeks, you are probably in the normal adjustment category. If you have symptoms which have persisted for more than three or four weeks or have recently worsened, you may be moving into the category of a postpartum clinical condition. Chapter eight offers detailed explanations of the clinical conditions on the rest of this spectrum, so turn to that chapter for help in evaluating your reactions.

5

Surviving the "Normal Crazy" of Postpartum Changes: Physical and Emotional Symptoms

The Short Version
(If You're Pressed For Time)

It's time now to take stock of exactly what you're experiencing and how much your symptoms—physical or emotional—are getting in the way of how you want to live. This chapter is designed to help you evaluate your feelings and symptoms and develop a plan of action that will help you feel better.

If you skipped chapter two, return to that chapter now and read about the self-care plan. The self-care plan is the foundation not only for prevention but for feeling better as well. Following the steps in that plan may offer some symptom relief so that you can address the other issues affecting your postpartum emotions. Once you have your self-care plan in place and are working to care for yourself, you may begin to feel better. Helpful techniques to address some of the most common physical and emotional issues of normal postpartum adjustment are addressed in this chapter.

Many of the negative feelings and symptoms that have been plaguing you may not disappear just because you begin to focus on your own needs, as advised for prevention in chapter two. This chapter is devoted to more in-depth, concrete ideas about what you can do to tackle these problems. You may want to scan the index below.

Exercise:
Two Minutes for Yourself

Try to remember a day in your life when you felt happy, peaceful, and self-confident. It doesn't matter if the memory is recent or from long ago. If you don't have an actual memory to draw on, imagine what a day like this would look like. Are there people around or are you alone? Are you at the beach, in an office, on stage, snuggled in bed? Picture as vividly as possible the details of your surroundings. Use all five senses—identify sounds, smells, tastes, textures, and colors. Now pay attention to what your body feels like on this wonderful day. What is your breathing like? Can you feel your heartbeat? Are your shoulders relaxed? Can you feel your happiness clear to the tips of your fingers?

Now take a mental snapshot of this scene. You can return here whenever you need to take a break, whenever you need to feel refreshed and renewed. It only takes a few minutes. You only have to close your eyes and look at the snapshot again. It will all come flooding back to you: the sounds, colors, tastes, textures, and smells; the feelings of happiness, peace, and self-confidence radiating out into each part of your body. No one can take this away from you. It's yours to keep and to draw on whenever you are in need.

5

Surviving the "Normal Crazy" of Postpartum Changes: Physical and Emotional Symptoms

Taking Care of Yourself

You may have become accustomed to taking good care of yourself physically while you were pregnant. During the last month of your pregnancy, you were probably weighed, examined, and encouraged by your doctor at least once a week. Many women try to eat right, exercise, and get sufficient rest while they're pregnant, spurred on by this attention to their body and the sense that more than their own health and well-being is on the line.

Once the baby has arrived, though, no one pays much attention to the new mom's body any more. Apart from your six-week doctor's visit you're more or less on your own. In fact, people may make a point of not talking about your body as it's probably looking and feeling a little out of shape right now. All those virtuous habits of self-care go flying out the window. Granted, time constraints and decreased energy make it difficult to keep up (or establish) a routine of exercise, rest, and healthy eating. Everyone's attention, including yours, shifts to the baby. It's the baby who gets weighed, measured, and cared for at each doctor's visit now, not you. With the focus no longer on your behavior, your needs seem much less important. No one fusses over you. Everyone fusses over the baby. Get the message? Besides, taking care of yourself physically is hard work. It would seem selfish, at this point, when your baby needs every minute of your attention, right?

These common misconceptions lay the foundation for many a new mother lapsing into complete neglect of her own needs in favor of those of the baby. This model of maternal self-sacrifice is rampant in our culture. Many of us were raised by mothers who were devoted to this ideal. As we said in previous chapters, this self-sacrificing model is not healthy or functional. Discard that model in favor of a healthier view. Consult chapter three for ideas on defeating these obstacles to self-care.

Is Your Pitcher Empty or Full?

Remember our image of a pitcher of water from chapter two? No one is a bottomless pitcher. If you do not designate time and energy to do what makes you feel well, rested, and happy, you will not have energy to meet the needs of those you love. What do you need in order to fill the pitcher again?

Begin with your physical needs. Continue to take your prenatal vitamins, eat nutritious meals, squeeze in some exercise, get as much rest/sleep/relaxation as you possibly can.

Don't neglect the emotional side of the equation. You truly need to talk with others in your same situation, to spend time and share tenderness with your spouse, to have a good laugh, to find at least a small bit of time for activities that gave you pleasure in your pre-baby days. You also need praise, from yourself as well as others, for the job you're doing. Give yourself a pat on the back. Ask explicitly for encouragement from your partner, other relatives, the pediatrician, or your friends.

It's impossible to be a good parent to your child if all your own needs go unmet. Give yourself permission to go to the well to refill your pitcher. Value yourself enough to ask others to give you what you need. If the "selfish" label keeps jumping up in your brain, remind yourself that this policy is like insurance or a savings account. You might prefer to use the money (or energy) now on something else, but down the road you'll be glad you invested (in yourself) for your child.

A further benefit of taking care of your own needs is the signal that you give to others. When you take care of yourself, other people treat you — and your needs — with respect. If you have a daughter, you will be providing her with a healthier role model than that of the self-sacrificing mother. If you have a son, you'll be giving him a valuable lesson about the way in which women should be treated and valued (your future daughter-in-law will thank you)!

The rest of this chapter is devoted to the ways in which you can keep your pitcher filled, coping with normal physical and emotional changes, so that you can be the sort of giving person you want to be.

Personalizing Your Survival Plan

Your survival plan began with the self-care steps outlined in chapter two. Hopefully, you have laid a good foundation of self-care that is helping balance your new life. By adding specific strategies targeted to your symptoms from this chapter you may begin to feel even better.

We know from experience that some problems require a more specific plan of action. After you've given the recommendations in chapter two your best shot, read our suggestions below for dealing with the other common complaints and symptoms. Scan the index in the short version of this chapter first and make check marks by the relevant symptoms. Then read one group of suggestions at a time. Give yourself the chance to absorb these ideas in a leisurely fashion. There's no quick fix for postpartum adjustment problems. You won't be able to address all your symptoms at once. Just deal with one item at a time — each a step toward feeling better.

How to Cope with Particular Symptoms

Thirty years ago, women spent at least a week in the hospital after having a baby. But over time, expectations and insurance regulations have changed. New mothers are no longer given much time to recover, either in the hospital or at home. Sometimes it helps to have explicit permission to take care of yourself physically. You may need to plan your day to include naps, exercise, and physical pampering. Soaking in the bathtub or treating yourself to a massage, professional or otherwise, can be extremely comforting. Your diet is important, especially those vitamins and minerals that are depleted by pregnancy, childbirth, and lactation. Taking care of yourself physically is one way to say, "I'm important — my health matters."

Before you head into our descriptions of specific symptoms and solutions, make sure you've read and worked on the basic foundation for self-care described in chapter two. It's almost impossible to relieve particular symptoms if you're not getting adequate rest, nutrition, and emotional nurturing. Add the suggestions listed here only after your primary needs have been addressed. Your healthcare provider should check out any persistent physical symptoms. You don't want to miss an underlying medical problem. If you've been given a clean bill of health, and still have symptoms, try some of the ideas from the list below.

Physical Symptoms

Low energy and fatigue. The lack of energy and extreme fatigue felt by many new mothers is due in large part to sleep deprivation and hormonal imbalances. You probably won't feel fully restored until a certain amount of time passes postpartum. The amount of time depends on your physical condition and the nature of your birth experience. However, certain measures can help.

The old advice to sleep when your baby sleeps is still good advice, even though it can be hard to follow. If you can't sleep, don't stress! At least designate a rest period of twenty minutes or so to put your feet up with a tall glass of water, juice, or herbal tea within easy reach. Listen to music or read something enjoyable. Do not do chores— remember that this is your official break time. The more you run around, the more stressed and depleted you'll feel. If your baby doesn't sleep sufficiently during the day to allow you to rest, call on your support network to relieve you. Ask someone else to take the baby out in her stroller or rock him while you take a nap or relax.

It may seem illogical, but exercise is also an excellent way to gain more energy. With your weary body, it may take a big push to get yourself moving. The payoff in energy is well worth the effort. Walking is probably the best thing you can do now. You can build your endurance gradually, you can take your baby with you, and you'll both get fresh air. If the weather's horrible, see if you can find a gym that has an indoor track, or a mall that allows walkers in before or after store hours. As soon as your OB gives you the okay, swimming is also a great way to regain your strength, although you'll have to get someone else to watch the baby.

Pay attention to your diet as well. Prepare or plan what you will eat in advance, or even better, let others prepare food for you. If you have a doughnut for breakfast and then feel exhausted by mid-morning, you're probably having a sugar crash. Make time to eat, for no fuel at all is even worse than that sugar crash. You need a balanced diet including low-fat sources of protein. Try to eat lots of fresh fruits, vegetables and whole grains such as brown rice, oats, and barley. Even if this isn't a diet you're accustomed to, it's one that will keep your system in working order. Snacking on nutritious foods throughout the day—having six small meals—is actually better for you than three full meals, which may be harder to digest.

A fun activity, or good talk with a friend, can also be energizing. If you're running on empty, and not taking some time for yourself, it's no wonder if you feel burned out and tired. If your fatigue is due to sleep problems read the next section.

Sleep problems. Sleep problems can take many forms: difficulty falling asleep, either at the start of the evening or after waking to feed the baby, early morning awakening, insomnia, or oversleeping. If you have trouble falling asleep, check out physical causes first. Caffeine (from coffee, soft drinks, tea, or chocolate) is the most common cause. Many new moms try to exist on sugar and caffeine. While these do keep you pumped up, they certainly are not physically sustaining. Having a glass of wine or another alcoholic beverage to try to ease yourself into sleep often backfires: the alcohol may relax you at first, but then acts as a stimulant a few hours later. Medications can keep you from sleeping well; talk with your doctor or pharmacist if you suspect that a drug you're taking is disturbing your sleep. Spicy foods or late-night snacks often interfere with dozing off.

If you have ruled out stimulants and you're still not sleeping, try to notice what you're thinking about when you lie awake. Anxiety and worry may be the main cause of insomnia in new mothers. See the suggestions later in this chapter for dealing with anxiety.

If you're not getting adequate sleep, you're probably getting more and more worried about how you'll get through the following day and how you will ever sleep the next night. Such worry can set up a vicious cycle of anxiety and sleeplessness. It may help to remember that lack of sleep, while tiring and annoying, is not life-threatening. To tackle insomnia, try to follow these guidelines:

- Stick to a regular schedule, especially a waking time. This can help reset your biological clock if it's gone haywire.
- Avoid naps if you're unable to sleep at night. Rest and relax instead.
- Avoid sleep-disruptive drugs and other stimulants such as caffeine.
- Exercise in the morning or early afternoon, not late in the day.
- Avoid heavy meals or feeling hungry close to bedtime.
- Sleep in a safe, secure, and quiet setting.

- Don't lie in bed for extended periods when you're not intending to sleep. Don't use your bed as a library or an office. Cultivate a strong association in your mind between going to bed and going to sleep.
- Try to wind down and relax in the evening. (This may be difficult if your baby tends to be fussy in the evening. If this is the case, try to get people in your support network to help out in the evening so that you can get some time to relax).
- Go to bed only when you're sleepy. However, try to keep to the same schedule every day.
- If you are not asleep ten to fifteen minutes after lying down, go into another room. Do something sleep-inducing or relaxing. Listen to music, read a boring book, listen to a relaxation tape, or imagine a blank screen in your head. Return to bed only when you are sleepy. Again, the goal is to associate your bed with falling asleep quickly. Repeat this process if necessary.
- Make it your goal to stay relaxed, rather than focus on falling asleep. Visualize a picture of a restful beach scene or similar place you love to help you relax.
- To wind down in the evening, practice slow, deep breathing. Breathe in and out so that your abdomen rises and falls. Watch the second hand on a clock. Inhale for three seconds, then exhale for six seconds.
- Have a glass of warm milk or a high carbohydrate snack (such as bread, cereal, bagel, or pasta). Turkey, chamomile, and apple juice are also natural sedatives.
- Soak in the bathtub or take a warm shower before going to bed.
- Set your alarm clock, but turn the clock around so you can't watch it.
- Get up at the same time every day.

If your problem is oversleeping (if you can't get up in the morning or you nap all day) a regular sleep schedule will help you as well. Exercise can energize you, as can high-protein snacks. Not being able to get up may be a sign of depression that you cannot easily tackle on your own. If this applies to you, please see the section in chapter ten on seeking professional help.

Appetite or eating changes. You may find that you suddenly have cravings or no appetite at all. Keep in mind that a well-balanced diet is essential to your physical and emotional health. Review the nutrition guidelines in chapter two on self-care basics. Often new moms neglect eating because they feel so pressed for time, then find themselves binging on what's easiest to grab. Usually, this means carbs and high-sugar foods or caffeine. Avoid this rut by eating small, fairly healthy meals at three to four hour intervals. Keep string cheese, fresh fruit, sliced turkey, low-fat yogurt and higher energy snacks such as nuts or protein bars on hand. Likewise, allow yourself reasonable portions of the foods you crave. Often, denial of the craved food only makes the craving worse.

Make sure you get adequate portions of all the nutrients you need. If you're nursing, you'll need 300 to 500 extra calories a day. Get nutritional advice from your doctor or La Leche League, or make an appointment to speak to a professional nutritionist. You'll probably be able to differentiate between cravings for particular foods — tomatoes or sushi, for instance — and an insatiable appetite. If you think you're eating mostly out of emotional need, follow the steps on self-care basics in chapter two to replenish yourself. If your eating is still out of control or you have a history of eating problems, consider seeking professional help (see chapter ten).

If you have no appetite, work on identifying a few foods that might taste good. Comfort foods, which you ate happily in childhood or at other times you recall fondly, are a good place to start. Maybe you can eat small amounts of soup, for instance, gradually adding bread or fruit to broaden your diet. Again, eating smaller amounts of food at three to four hour intervals may work best. Say, "I'm eating so I can care for my baby." If you find that you cannot force yourself to eat, have persistent worries about choking when you eat, have recurring nausea, or you're throwing up after you eat, get professional help right away.

Hyperactivity. Perhaps you feel driven to accomplish everything. You can't stop and rest; you feel very jumpy inside. If you can, force yourself to take rest times. Breathe deeply and reduce the number of tasks you are trying to accomplish. Make sure you are exercising. Watch your intake of caffeine and sugar; both of these substances can hype you up. Many new moms rely on these for energy, and don't or won't take the time to eat a nutritious snack or meal. If you cannot make yourself slow down, you must seek professional help. You may be experiencing postpartum mania and may be at risk for a more serious postpartum clinical condition.

Physical symptoms of stress and anxiety. Stress and anxiety are frequently experienced as physical symptoms, especially postpartum due to hormonal and other physiologic changes. Some common signs are: lightheadedness, butterflies, feeling jittery, itchy skin, dizziness, hot or cold flashes, constipation and diarrhea. Like other normal postpartum changes, these are best diminished by practicing self-care with sound physical, emotional and social nourishment. Refer to chapter two for specific guidelines.

If you're following the recommendations in chapter two and symptoms persist, then you may be developing clinical anxiety. Hyperventilation, dizziness, shaking, hot or cold flashes, numbness or tingling, and heart palpitations can all be signs of a panic attack. In addition to physical concerns, moms worry they are having a heart attack or going crazy. Panic attacks are triggered by biological changes and can be treated medically. It's important to seek treatment early because the longer panic attacks continue, the more likely that your body can develop a habit of responding in this reactive way. See the section later on anxiety, worry, or obsessive thoughts.

Emotional Symptoms

Crying. Crying and tearfulness in the postpartum period can have any number of causes. Tears can come from feeling overwhelmed, tired, frustrated, depleted, hungry, or sleepy. You may feel a sense of loss about any number of issues. You may miss your life as it was before the baby came. You might resent the contrast between your dreams of the perfect baby or delivery and the way things turned out. You mourn your pre-baby figure and how long it's taking you to lose the weight you gained during pregnancy. Address each of these underlying causes. Read the recommendations for sleep problems above, or sections on loss in chapter six and trouble coping later in this chapter.

If none of these issues seem to strike a chord for you, and/or you just feel like crying, go ahead and cry. Crying can be beneficial in releasing stress. Set aside fifteen or twenty minutes each day to cry out your feelings. Set the kitchen timer, collect the tissues, and cry. Or cry in the shower. If you fear you will not be able to stop once you begin, setting the timer or an alarm clock, and planning an activity (exercise, a shower, a call to a friend) for when your crying session ends can enable you to take control. If you find that you cannot truly control the crying in this way, see the chapter on getting professional help (chapter ten).

Lack of confidence, feelings of inadequacy. Few people feel like a parent when they take that new baby home. If you find yourself saying, "Where did this baby come from, and what am I supposed to do with him?" you are completely normal. It's a myth that you will suddenly know what your baby needs, or what you have to do to feel like a parent. Reassure yourself, your partner, your baby, and your family (if they ask) that you certainly can learn to fulfill your role as a parent. What is important is that you know you can and that you tell yourself this. Write it down and post it on notes around the house if you need reassurance: "I can be a good parent." "I can be a person and a parent, too." Read these affirmations to yourself at various times throughout the day. Do some research if this will reassure you. Talk to friends or relatives about their parenting styles; scan some books or parenting websites. Find out what feels right to you. There are endless styles and answers to parenting questions. Give yourself permission to find a style that suits you. Take as much time as you need to develop it. Good parenting is an art, not an exact science. What works for one child and one family may not work for another. There is no single right way. Write down what you are doing right, such as comforting or smiling at your baby. Take a parenting course if this will boost your confidence, or call a parent information hotline if you need specific answers right now. Keep telling yourself, "I can do this." Like any new task, confidence builds with time.

Sadness. Feelings of sadness tend to well up easily in the postpartum period. This might seem strange to you in the context of everyone saying, "Lucky you—this is the happiest time of your life!" Expectations that your life should be wonderful now only make you feel worse, making you wonder, "What's the matter with me?" In reality, it's not uncommon to feel sad when you have a new baby. If you can identify some of the reasons underlying your sadness, list them on a piece of paper or talk about them with your partner or a trusted friend. Allow yourself to feel sad and ask others to reinforce this permission, telling you it's okay to feel your feelings. If you can pinpoint specific causes, evaluate whether there are problems that can be solved or if there's a situation you need to grieve. If your unhappiness stems from something that's changeable, define the change you'd like to see and make a plan for moving toward that goal. If you're dealing with a condition that is not likely to change, see the entry on loss in chapter six.

Irritability or hypersensitivity. Fluctuating hormones, fatigue, and the uncertainties that go with being a new parent all contribute to the irritability and hypersensitivity that new mothers often feel. Take a look at when your feelings get hurt most quickly, and see if any patterns exist. Does it happen when you are tired, hungry, or when you've been alone all day? Is it worse in the evening when you are looking forward to your partner's return, and your expectations of relief are high? If you can see factors that trigger your irritability, work to change them. If your partner wants to come home and play with the baby, leaving you feeling neglected, speak up. Give yourself permission to ask for some attention, too. If you're feeling overwhelmed, see the entry in this chapter on trouble coping, feeling overwhelmed or powerless. Often it helps to write down your feelings in a journal or letter. Having an outlet for negative feelings makes them less powerful. Clear communication can take away some of the hurt. If you feel that someone is criticizing your behavior, go ahead and ask him/her to reword his/her statement. If your spouse comes in at the end of the day and says, "You're still in your nightgown!" it might sound like he's saying, "What did you do all day?" Asking him to clarify what he means might reveal that he really wanted to say, "You poor dear! Was it rough today?" If he was taking you to task for not getting dressed, let him know more of the details of your day so that he can develop a little more empathy. Tell him clearly that you don't have any tolerance for criticism now; you're feeling insecure enough as it is. Tell him and others around you that, for now especially, you need to hear supportive statements and encouragement.

Taking several deep breaths and counting to ten are old standbys for preventing an all-out fight. When you give yourself time to think through what bothered you about another person's comment, you can evaluate whether your perceptions are accurate and fair. You may be able to respond in a more measured and reasonable way. Some people are simply toxic in the amount of criticism they deal out or in the way they play on your insecurities. It may be necessary to steer clear of these people while you're in such a vulnerable state, no matter who they are, whether it's your mother, your sister-in-law, or your nearest neighbor. If it's your partner who's pressing your buttons, try to convince him to enter couples therapy with you.

NOTE: Intense irritability or hypersensitivity coupled with difficulty sleeping or eating could be symptoms of mania. If you are having moderate to severe irritability or hypersensitivity along with eating or sleeping problems, please see your healthcare provider right away.

Anger. Anger may be the feeling that you least expected to have after the birth of your baby. What on earth do you have to feel angry about? you may ask yourself. Others may even ask you that question. Rest assured that anger is a common and normal postpartum emotion for many women. It may seem incredibly strong.

There are legitimate reasons to be angry after having a baby. Most of them have to do with expectations. You did not expect to feel so badly. You did not expect to feel so out of control. You did not expect your baby to cry all the time, or be a boy, or girl, or look like your father, or be sick, or colicky, or any number of other things that have come to pass. You did not expect to have the birth experience you had. You did not expect to feel neglected by your partner, parent, or friend. You expected your loved ones to be more helpful and involved. You expected to get some rest and to look and feel better sooner. You may feel cheated about any number of things. While you may be surprised about having these feelings, there's nothing wrong with you for feeling them. You are not crazy.

However, you may need to adjust your expectations a bit. See the sections on trouble coping, feeling overwhelmed or powerless that follow, and in chapter six on control and perfectionism. The entries in chapter six on dysfunctional family of origin, uninvolved or absent partner, loss, and relationship difficulties may be helpful as well.

You may need to find a safe outlet for your anger. If you push your anger down inside you and deny or minimize its importance, you're more likely to explode over some minor hurt or insult. Such an explosion can blow everything out of proportion. You may feel as though you've lost your credibility as a reasonable person. It may also make you feel uncomfortably out of control.

Try getting out your anger in some physical way. Exercise, jump rope, punch a pillow, throw or kick a ball, break eggs in the sink, blow up a paper bag and pop it. Take a shower and scream in the shower or scream in your car with all the windows rolled up. Or scream silently: clench your fists, tense your shoulders, prepare to scream but let only the air, not the noise, out of your mouth. You may find relief in writing your feelings in a journal or scribbling them on paper. Tearing paper or phone books can relieve lots of anger and tension. Make angry faces in the mirror. Go out in the backyard and stomp around. Hit a plastic bat against the fence. Make a list of what anger activities work for you. Keep it handy so that you can easily pick one when you feel you're about to explode. If anger is a problem for you, try to do some of the things on the list every day, even before you feel ready to explode. Consider it insurance.

Note: If you feel you cannot control your anger and may hurt yourself or others, please seek immediate professional help.

Speaking up is also an important way to diffuse anger. Keep in mind that you want your expression of angry feelings to be assertive, not aggressive. You want to speak your mind without hurting others. Use the word "I" rather than "you." Avoid name-calling or accusations. Stick to the event at hand, rather than the last 40 anger-provoking events in your life. For example, say, "I was angry when you walked in and right past me to the baby. I want you to greet me first." This will get you to a solution much more quickly than saying, "You are so heartless! You ignore me all the time." Try to be specific about what was done and what you would like to have done differently. Realize that you have a right to express your angry feelings, but so does the other person. Be prepared to listen and to acknowledge the other person's feelings. "I didn't know you were angry, too," can go a long way toward soothing someone's feelings. Finally, expressing your anger may not accomplish anything more than making you feel better by getting the anger off your chest. Keep your expectations in check here, too. Remember that you're expressing your anger as a way to make yourself feel better. You're not getting your anger out to make someone else feel guilty or as a way to control someone. Change may come about as a result of your words, but there are no guarantees.

Confusion or trouble with concentration. It's common in the postpartum period for new mothers to feel "muddled." You may lose your train of thought, forget what you were going to say or do, or even become confused about what day of the week it is. This muddled state of mind is likely caused by a combination of fatigue, concentration on the new job of being a parent, and fluctuating hormones. To remedy this, first make sure that your habits for rest, relaxation, and diet are in good shape. Try to decrease overload and expectations. Having fewer jobs to keep track of will help. Make lists and write things down but keep your lists simple. Many women find it most useful to make their (brief) lists the night before, rather than in the morning when they're feeling groggy. Pick your most alert time and plan your day then. Using a calendar with reminders and checking off each day can orient you about the passage of time. Take rest breaks. When you close your eyes briefly, use your imagination like a TV screen to focus on important tasks or items to remember. If your partner or family members are more organized than you're feeling now, let them call you or write you notes with daily reminders. (Avoid this if their reminders feel more like pressure than help—stay attuned to what works for you). Talking to yourself, naming the task at hand or item to remember, can help you stay focused. If you forget why you went to the baby's room, recite while you're walking there the next time: "I am going to get the blanket, I am going to get the blanket." This may feel strange at first but it will put you back in control. If feelings are getting in the way and interfering with your concentration, attend to those feelings. (See the relevant entries in this chapter on anxiety, worry, and obsessive thoughts; sadness, hopelessness, and trouble coping, feeling overwhelmed or powerless, or on loss in the next chapter). If you are so confused that you cannot complete simple tasks or care for yourself or the baby, seek professional help (see chapter ten).

Trouble coping, feeling overwhelmed or powerless. Everything may be feeling as if it's crashing in on you. You can't get anything done. You feel as if you have little or no control over the day's events and your reactions to them.

First of all, single out one area in which you do have control. Certainly you are accomplishing *something*. This may be as simple as getting the baby's diaper changed when needed. You are succeeding here. Write this down on a note card and post it somewhere: "I am getting the baby's diapers changed every day." Pat yourself on the back. Reassure yourself that there is nothing wrong with you for feeling overwhelmed with your life. Adjusting to a new baby and accomplishing all the work involved is a mammoth task. You do have control in some areas, though, so exercise that control. Make the bed every day or clean one room and keep it clean, free of baby paraphernalia. Decide on one task you will do per day and get that one task done, even if it is only feeding the baby or getting your shower. Slowly add one more task at a time, working toward only what you can reasonably hope to accomplish. Sit down with your partner or a trusted friend or family member and examine your expectations.

Throw out any expectations that are unrealistic. Brainstorm about ways to get help with basic chores—things that will make your life miserable if they're left undone. Can you afford to hire someone to help clean your house? Is there someone in your support network who will shop for you until you're able to handle the shopping? Can you and your partner eat nutritious take-out food a few times a week to cut down on the cooking and shopping until you're feeling better? Can you lower your housekeeping standards until you have more time? Take things one day at a time, and focus on the tasks you manage to accomplish—not on everything that's still not done. Keep in mind that the chaos in your life now is temporary.

Guilt. The adjustment to parenthood is often complicated by guilt. It's a difficult task to try to maintain your pre-baby life and do a good job of meeting your baby's needs as well. You may feel as if you never have enough time for everything you want to do. If you neglect your own needs or your partner or your job, you feel guilty. And you feel guilty if you put any of those priorities above the baby's needs.

Guilt just comes with the territory at times. It's normal to want to be at home with the baby if you're at work and to want a break from the baby if you're at home. Getting yourself on a schedule so that time is allotted for everyone's needs (including your own) can help. Play with the baby, then do one household task. Next take a brief rest break for yourself followed by cuddle time for your partner. Of course, your schedule will be determined by how cooperative or sleepy your baby is, or on the strength and presence of your support network. You can tell yourself that you are doing it all, just not all at once.

What you say to yourself is equally important in combating mother guilt. Focus on what you have accomplished rather than on what you had to leave undone. State your accomplishments out loud to yourself. "I got the beds made." "I snuggled with the baby." "I'm doing a decent job with the housework." "I completed that project on time." Specific accomplishments listed on a piece of paper on your desk or the fridge can remind you that you are making progress. You also may need to lower your standards and set less ambitious goals for a while.

To deal with guilt, social support is again critical. If you are at home, find other at-home parents to meet with on a regular basis. If you're working out of the home, join a women's organization and find some other working mothers, allowing you to compare notes.

Hopelessness. Hopelessness is a sign that should not be ignored. You may feel you will never have your old life back. You may feel you have made a serious mistake in becoming a parent. You may have a vague sense that your life is over or that you can never be a good parent. If you have identified causes, work to take control of the parts you can change. Look each day for one small glimmer of hope that the situation really does have potential to change. In a notebook, record each sign that you are moving in the right direction. Read the entries nightly. See the entry earlier on trouble coping, feeling overwhelmed or powerless. If you feel unable to tackle your feelings of hopelessness, see chapter ten on getting professional help.

A lack of feeling toward the baby, anger, or over-protectiveness. The idea that bonding takes place on the birthing bed is an old myth that refuses to die. The attachment process is a slow, gradual growth of feeling between you and your baby. As you get to know your child, your emotions will evolve. Anger or overprotectiveness toward your baby may occur as you become attached for many reasons. You may spend more time with the baby than with any other person. The baby may be the source of most of your joy as well as your frustration with your life right now. After all, you did not feel this way before the baby appeared. Read the entries in this chapter on worry, anxiety, or obsessive thoughts and anger.

Worry, anxiety, or obsessive thoughts. You may find that you are stuck on certain worries or thoughts that make you feel anxious. Anxiety and worry frequently plague new parents. Surviving pregnancy and childbirth may give you a new awareness of the fragile nature of human life. You see how small and vulnerable your baby seems. Naturally, you are inclined to protect him or her. Given the world of violence and potential harm we live in, it is quite natural to wonder (and worry) about how infants ever grow to reach adulthood. Then for you to be in charge-how overwhelming!

You can't protect your child from every danger in the world. On the other hand, not all those threats come barging in the door at once, either. You'll have time to teach your child, as best you can, to live as wisely and safely as possible. In the meantime it's your job to protect your baby for the next few years. You cannot protect your baby perfectly. No parent is all-powerful.

Many events that affect your child are simply not subject to your control. You can't control weather or wars or an uneven pavement that may cause your child to trip and fall. You can't shield your child from every disease-bearing cough, sneeze, or handshake. To manage your worries and anxieties, you can first make sure you're taking all the recommended steps to care for your child. Use a car seat, keep vaccinations up to date, feed her well, make sure no one smokes in your household. Tell yourself, "I'm controlling what I can."

For your own peace of mind, you may want to quit reading the news in the paper or online, or watching the evening news or talk shows for a while. It can be helpful to have a "worry time" set aside each day. Keep a tablet close by throughout the day. Record worries as they pop into your brain. Set them aside for the designated time. Then focus on the worries, problem-solving if you can, for ten minutes. At the end of that time, set the tablet out of view. Repeat at intervals throughout the day if needed.

Obsessive thoughts are thoughts or ideas that occur again and again. Many women experience obsessive thoughts about harm that could come to the baby or other loved ones. You may find yourself thinking about throwing the baby down the stairs, hurting the baby with knives, or fearing that the baby will contract a horrific disease. A new mother will often feel as if these thoughts come from nowhere and that she's unable to control or stop them. Often writing these thoughts provides relief. Try to let the thoughts just "pass through" your brain. Tell yourself that these are just thoughts. No need to act on them. You may have had lots of thoughts in your life that you chose not to act upon. Another helpful fact to dwell on is that these thoughts are simple manifestations of a chemical imbalance in your brain. They are not the "true you," only now surfacing. They are not reality. They mean nothing about you as a person or a mom. They are just blips on the screen of your brain. Treat them like pop-up ads on your web browser: shut them down, close them out; they are of little consequence.

Women who have obsessive thoughts are keenly aware of the importance of their new role as a parent. You may be particularly sensitive to how fragile life is and how vulnerable your child is. These obsessive thoughts may be one way that your body keeps you attuned to that vulnerability, so you will remain vigilant about your child's safety. However, this can get out of control; you may focus too much on the dangers your child faces in this world rather than on the control you do have. Talk to a knowledgeable professional if you feel you cannot see anything ahead but danger for your child.

Along with these thoughts, which for most women feel uncontrollable, often comes extreme guilt. "What is the matter with me for having such thoughts?" you may ask yourself in horror. It may help to know that women who have such thoughts rarely act on them. You also need to tell yourself that having these thoughts does not mean that you intend to act on them. If you have repetitive thoughts of harm, the section on guilt in this chapter may be helpful. You may wish to find someone to talk to who has experienced similar obsessive thoughts. You may be able to find a postpartum support group, or a telephone volunteer (through P.S.I. —see the resources section) who can reassure you.

It's important to make sure that you have obsessive-compulsive disorder rather than psychosis. Chapter eight makes these distinctions clear. If you, or anyone around you, has doubts about your status, please consult with a medical professional with knowledge about these clinical conditions. Obsessive-compulsive disorder is biologically caused and responds to medication. Cognitive behavioral therapy is also extremely effective. Refer to chapter ten.

6

Surviving Postpartum Challenges:
New Mom Issues and Answers

You have worked very hard to lay out your self-care plan, outlined in chapter two. In chapter five, you looked at ways to cope with the physical and emotional reactions, or symptoms, that comprise the "normal crazy" many new mothers experience. Chapter five offered concrete tools to expand your self-care plan, targeting the specific reactions you may be having. In this chapter, common underlying issues that plague new moms are described. Answers to address these issues are offered. By applying the coping strategies here for an issue that plagues you, you may be better able to keep your emotional balance. Consider the ideas in this chapter as more tricks in your tool box to prevent postpartum depression and anxiety and/or help relieve symptoms as they develop. The issues and accompanying answers contained in this chapter are listed in the index below. Read any that seem to fit for your life.

Exercise:
Two Minutes for Yourself

Imagine you have a magic wand. Wave it in the air. What five most pressing things would you change in your life? Write these down in order of importance, listing your highest priority first. Now focus on the top item. Where could you begin to bring about a change in this matter? Think of just one thing you could begin to do *today* that would make a difference. Do that one thing. For example, you may have written, "My relationship is falling apart." What would make you feel that things between you and your partner were getting better? Maybe you two could sit down and talk together for five minutes tonight after the baby is asleep. Talk about something pleasant. Sit close. Remember why you liked each other in the first place. Share some memories about fun times you've shared. Tell each other a secret.

6

Surviving Postpartum Challenges: New Mom Issues and Answers

Symptoms, described in chapter five, are actual physical and emotional changes you may have in the postpartum period. Issues, on the other hand, are the underlying concerns that may lead to those symptoms. Often, formulating a survival plan that just focuses on symptoms is not enough. Rather, most new mothers need to pay attention to the feelings and changes required of them as they adjust to this new baby. This section can help you identify and sort out the major effects the birth of your child has had on your life.

Social support or social withdrawal. Whether you know and talk often with other people who have babies can make a big difference in your life postpartum. Research has shown that new parents who talk regularly with a person who understands their trials and joys have an easier adjustment than do new parents without such friends. Making new friends, or time for the ones you do have, can seem impossible when you have a new baby and can barely get yourself dressed each day. Making friends as an adult isn't as easy as it was in childhood or college days, when there was a ready supply of prospects at school. At a younger age, you may have felt more open emotionally and more willing to take risks. You may know few women on your block who stay at home or no coworkers with children. If you need to find potential friends, getting out and approaching other mothers you see is essential. Speak to them in the grocery store or the park. Advertise at your pediatrician's office or your place of worship. Take a postpartum exercise class or a mom-baby class at your local recreation center. Check with your local hospital, mental health association, place of worship or school district about new mother groups or mom-baby classes in your area.

Once you have spotted a person or two who is in the same boat, make getting to know that person a priority. If you already know another new mom, commit to meet with her on a regular basis. Plan a coffee break, start a play group or a babysitting co-op, schedule a daily walk, or take an exercise class together. Even planning a daily talk on the phone with friends can provide a much-needed opportunity to compare notes, commiserate, and share solutions. You may have to work on keeping in touch with friends this way. Think of it as another habit that you want to develop in your determination to take care of yourself. Make it the one accomplishment, beyond basic baby care, that you mandate for each week.

Control and perfectionism. These may seem like two very different issues, but in practice they're intimately related. Control is a matter of wanting everything to be "the right way." This often translates into 1) wanting things to be perfect, and 2) wanting things to be a certain way. When you have a new baby, it's often difficult to accept the many aspects of your life that you can't control. Your life may no longer seem perfect, or as nearly perfect as it was before. You can't make the baby sleep. You can't make yourself sleep at times. Often, you can't make the baby stop crying. You can't control what your partner does or says. He may not be the perfect parent you hoped he'd be. Your formerly lovely house may be a total mess with laundry, baby things, dirty dishes, and wilted flowers everywhere. This all may make you feel extremely out of control, as if you can influence nothing in your life.

Perhaps you've been accustomed to controlling your life to a great extent. You may have finished your education, delaying marriage and having a baby until the time was right. This may mean that you had finally bought a home, or had planned the baby for a certain time of year or had saved enough money so that you could stay home with the baby for several years. The cold, cruel reality of not being able to control your life to this extent anymore may now be hitting you hard. It may be time to adjust your expectations. Time to identify those issues that you can control in your life right now. You have to choose your battles from now on. Some things may just have to go so that you can relax and enjoy life more. You can't control the baby and her schedule any more than you can make your partner do things your way. Often, making a conscious decision to let go and give up control over everything (a futile goal, anyway) can be helpful. Tell yourself, "I can't make everything perfect," or "I need to let go of what I can't change." Give yourself permission to no longer be the one in charge of everything and everybody.

You may need to push yourself to make mistakes in order to have a chance to accept them. You will not know that mistakes and imperfection are tolerable, and not life-threatening, unless you actually make them. Experiment with some little things. Put the baby's shirt on backwards or inside-out. If you are picking up the toys (or clothes or books and papers) every time the baby goes to sleep, practice leaving them out until day's end instead. Don't wear make-up one day. Serve cereal for dinner. All of these small imperfections can broaden your perspective. You slacked off and life went on. Pick some mistakes you can tolerate. Work your way up to bigger ones. (However, don't lose sight of things that are critical. You still need to pay bills on time, drive the speed limit, and change the baby's diaper when it's soiled).

While you are working on making little mistakes, pay attention to what goes on in your head. Remember, your emotions are linked to what you say when you talk to yourself. You'll feel better if your self-talk is positive, rather than negative or toxic. Remind yourself that you are being a good parent or partner. Make up some positive affirmations: "I am a worthwhile person who sometimes makes mistakes." "I'm a loving mother, and I'm doing the best I can right now." Write them on note cards or self-adhesive notes. Post your notes on your mirror, above the changing table, on your dashboard, or on the refrigerator door. When you read them, practice thinking about yourself in a different way. You can do things imperfectly, leave some tasks undone, and still be an immensely valuable person. That baby of yours doesn't care if the bed is made or the towels match. You still love the other imperfect people in your life, in spite of their human flaws. Extend this same kindness to yourself.

You may want to refer back to the entry in chapter five on trouble coping, feeling overwhelmed or powerless for more ideas on changing your perspective.

Dysfunctional family of origin. Perhaps in your family of origin your feelings were not respected or you were not allowed to be yourself. You may feel a deep hurt about wrongs inflicted on you by your family. Your parents may have provided models that you desperately don't want to copy. You may fear imposing their parenting style on your own child. There are many ways in which the family in which you grew up can influence your own transition to parenthood. You may feel a need to face those family issues once your own baby has arrived.

You may need to do some serious thinking about what needs to be different. If you had a magic wand, what would you change about your family or its influence at this time in your life? Once you can define a specific goal, such as, "My mother needs to tell me positive, not negative, things about my ability to be a parent," you can brainstorm about how you might achieve that goal. It is often easier to write letters to family members telling them what you would like to see change, rather than confronting them in person or by telephone. You may want to write several drafts of your letter. Have a trusted person review them for you and offer constructive criticism. You may also want to practice what you would say to family members, should they call you or talk to you in person in response to your letter. Rehearse in front of the mirror, keeping focused on your feelings. Use "I" rather than "you" in your sentences. Just like giving voice to your anger, it may be enough to identify and acknowledge your feelings without sharing them with others. You may want to wait until you are further along in your postpartum adjustment to share them.

Families can be powerful influences in our lives. It can be very difficult to sort these things out on your own. If confronting your family seems overwhelming, you may want to get the added support of professional counseling. An impartial third party may be better equipped than someone close to you to help you decide what changes you want to make. Many therapists are well-schooled in techniques to help you change the role you play in your family of origin. If you're worried about hurting family members by bringing up the issues involved, think about your problem from the perspective of a parent. If you were doing something that hurt your son or daughter, wouldn't you want your child to tell you so that you could make the situation better?

If your parents are deceased or otherwise unavailable, it's still important to work these issues out of your system. Write letters even if you can't mail them. Putting your thoughts down on paper can do wonders to clarify your feelings. The best insurance against repeating dysfunctional family patterns is to be as conscious and clear about them as possible, and then take steps to avoid repeating them. Read *The Dance of Anger* by Harriet Lerner, an excellent guide for changing family patterns.

Uninvolved or absent partner. In many marriages, one partner may in effect be absent because of work demands, travel schedules, or having a busy life in general. Perhaps you pictured parenting as a joint venture, but now feel as if you're flying solo. Some new mothers feel this way because of the physical demands of breastfeeding. Mothers, much more often than fathers, take extended leave for infant care. Even though times are changing, many new parents still must struggle consciously not to fall into the traditional roles of father as breadwinner and mother as homemaker. We've noticed a tendency in many new fathers to actually increase their time at work postpartum. This appears to be a common way for men to cope with the new responsibilities of being a parent (or adding a child to their family). In the words of one new father, "Suddenly I was responsible for another human being. I felt an overwhelming urge to make more money, work harder, save more to give my baby the best." Work may also provide an arena in which the new father feels in control, compared to the many unknowns of infant care at home. He may spend more time at work because it's familiar and therefore more comfortable. For these many reasons, you may find yourself shouldering what seems like the total burden of infant care and running the household.

There are techniques you can use to increase your partner's involvement with both you and the baby. You may want to begin by setting up a weekly "date." That might entail time out of the house for you and your partner together, dinner together after the baby is in bed, or simply a designated "talk time" to keep in touch with each other's lives. Your relationship is the foundation of your new family. You will now need to devote time to nurturing it, just as you need to nurture your baby. You need to plan time together; otherwise, it can easily get swallowed up by other tasks that seem much more pressing. Sitting together and just listening to music, cuddling, or taking turns massaging each other's shoulders are other important ways to stay close and keep in touch.

Assigning your partner one specific childcare task each day can also increase his involvement with the baby. You'll get a break as well. Have your partner give the baby a bath each evening or rock the baby to sleep. It's tempting to have your partner tackle the dishes, rather than an infant-care task. But your goal is to involve him with the baby and to build the infant-parent relationship, as well as to give you a break. Some new fathers may feel uncomfortable about their lack of experience with babies and may balk at taking on such a task. With time, they can develop confidence and may come to treasure their special time with their babies. You may have to "disappear" during this time. Go into your room and close the door, take a shower, go for a walk, or run an errand. Otherwise, you may be tempted to hover and offer comments on how to do the task the "right" way. Your way is not necessarily the only way. Your partner may feel comfortable with a different style. Experts say that babies benefit from the different approaches a mother and father bring to parenting. When you remain in the background directing the parent-child interaction, you may aggravate your partner's lack of self-confidence and actually discourage further involvement. All parents must find their own way to meet their baby's needs. If you correct your partner too much, you may find the whole load of responsibility back in your lap.

In addition to having your partner take charge of one specific task each day, you may want to schedule a morning or evening "off duty" for yourself each week. Your partner can take over then, giving you time for yourself. This is important even for parents who are working full-time. You may feel as if you're already gone too much. Remember that you're a person first and a parent second. You still need time to devote to non-parental interests. If setting up structured plans doesn't relieve negative feelings about your partner's absences or lack of emotional involvement you may want to consult a competent couple therapist.

If your child's father doesn't live with you, please read chapter seven, which addresses the special needs of single parents.

Loss. There are certain losses that are part of being a new parent. You may feel a real loss of freedom. You're no longer able to come and go as you please and always must plan for the baby before you go anywhere. You may feel sad about losing your carefree, childless lifestyle. Sleeping until noon on the weekends, staying up late, dancing until dawn may be luxuries of the past. Many women feel that they have lost their "self" and have turned into a parent, a person who is foreign to them. "I'm no longer the old me," is a frequent complaint. You may feel sad about losing the specialness of pregnancy. You are no longer the focus of attention and doting. People now smile at the baby, not you. You may feel the loss of the close relationship you had with your physician or midwife. You visit extensively with that person for nine months, trust in them, rely on them, feel cared for by them. Then suddenly that person is discharging you, and you will see them only rarely.

You need to allow yourself to acknowledge any losses that you feel keenly. They are real. Give yourself permission and time to grieve your losses. Acknowledge the sadness, cry, keep a journal to record your feelings. You need to seek the support of your family in this process as well. You may need to hear from your partner that the loss is real. This confirmation that you need to grieve can be the first step to feeling better. Don't be afraid to ask for this acknowledgement and support from the people who matter to you.

A death in the family, illness, or disability of any close relative, friend, or the baby can significantly affect your feelings postpartum. Other losses, such as moving to another state or town, changing jobs, or friends moving away can also feel devastating at this time. You may feel as if you should just cheer up and forget the loss, focus on the baby instead. You're even likely to hear such suggestions from well-meaning family or friends.

You need to allow yourself to feel your feelings rather than push them away. Give yourself permission to grieve. Cry, set aside time to feel sad, record your feelings in a journal or letters to loved ones. This is a real loss you have experienced, and you need to grieve it just as you would any other loss in your life. Just because you have a new baby doesn't mean that your feelings of grief are any different or any less powerful. It only means that the grief may be harder to face and you have less time to take care of your emotional needs. It's still essential that you find the time. It's important for those around you to realize that you need to grieve and for them to offer words of encouragement and support as you air your feelings.

If you find that you cannot grieve your losses on your own, you may wish to participate in a local grief group. Often sponsored by religious or mental health organizations, these groups work as classes, educating participants about the grief process. Having a specific time and place set aside to grieve, in a group like this, can make working through the grief an easier task. Professional counseling is another option for working through your feelings of loss.

Body image. Your body doesn't feel like yours anymore. You may look in the mirror and wonder who it is you're seeing. What happened to your pre-baby body? Just getting dressed in the morning can trigger all kinds of negative feelings about your current shape and weight. Exercise and proper diet are critical to feeling better, of course. Shop smart, stocking up on low-fat, high energy foods like whole-grain breads, nonfat yogurt, fruit, and vegetables. Plan special low-fat snacks for your break times. Make a point of using a special mug or napkin or setting a flower in a vase on the table. Take a postpartum exercise class where babies are welcome. Get back to an activity you enjoyed pre-baby, such as tennis, golf, or running.

Exercise and diet are important but so is what you say to yourself. Stating to yourself, or posting on your fridge, "My body is looking better and better every day," or "I can eat just what I need," can make you believe that you can control this part of your life. Look in the mirror and find one feature that you like in your appearance. Then celebrate it some way. Wear a shirt that matches your eyes. Buy a new clip for your hair. The next week, search for another feature you can feel good about right now. Set small goals, and focus on telling yourself you are doing well enough. Your body has changed and may never be exactly the same as it was before. You may need to grieve this as a significant loss (see the earlier entry on loss). Change what you can. Talk yourself into acceptance of what won't change. Your baby loves your body just the way it is.

Try to be loving toward yourself as well. If none of your clothes fit you, buy some attractive clothes that fit your body just as it is now. Don't put off looking your best until you have your old body back or lose a certain amount of weight. Celebrate your body as it is in the here and now. It's performed miraculous feats and deserves some positive recognition.

Financial stress. Changing income levels and rising expenses cause financial stress for many new parents. If you and your partner make an effort not to spend more than you take in, the financial strain of having a baby will probably diminish over time. Likewise, if you set your priorities on what is most important now (clothing your child versus buying that new car you have your eye on), choices may be easier. Giving up the lifestyle you've had may be difficult, but going into debt to hold onto it is not a satisfactory solution. Recognize that it's tough to resist the "have it now—consume, consume" mentality that this culture reinforces. If your financial problems seem overwhelming, you may want to find a nonprofit credit counseling service in your area for advice on budgeting and consolidation of debt.

Attachment. You may worry about the effects of your postpartum adjustment symptoms on the relationship you are developing with your baby. Attachment or bonding with your baby occurs over the course of time and is influenced by many factors. Your mood is just one of those factors. While you want to do all you can to take care of yourself and improve your mood, you need to remember that how you feel is not the only influence. Your baby's temperament, the involvement of other adults in your baby's life, and the interaction you and the baby have on your good days all affect the bonding process. The passage of time will help you build the relationship with your baby as you begin to feel better. There is no "critical period" for human infants when you two either have to bond or all is lost. If you miss the first few weeks of your child's life because of severe symptoms, you can work at the mother-infant relationship when you feel better.

You may feel simple concern about your relationship with the baby. Or you may feel that your baby is rejecting you or doesn't like you. Planning time to play with your baby or simply watching what your baby can do at different stages is helpful. Borrow or buy a book on what babies can do, such as *Baby Minds: Brain-Building Games Your Baby Will Love* by Linda Acredolo and Susan Goodwyn. Child development and childcare books and websites can give you ideas on how to approach your baby. You may need reassurance that your baby sees you as someone special. Ask your partner or the baby's pediatrician to help you identify the positive ways in which the baby responds to you, if you are unable to identify these on your own. Or have someone videotape an interaction between you and the baby, then watch it at a quiet time. This will allow you to see the baby's responses a bit more objectively, and will also allow you to gauge your own responses and body language.

Infant massage is another strategy for connecting with your baby. Many hospitals offer courses in infant massage for parents. Learning these skills takes only a few hours and has benefits beyond facilitating the attachment to your baby. Baby massage also calms fussy and difficult babies, making it easier to connect with them.

It takes a while for babies to begin responding differently to different people, especially if you're bottle-feeding. Be patient; give it time. Mental health professionals offer parent-child therapy to improve your attachment if you continue to be concerned about it. The family in which you grew up may be influencing your ability to bond with your baby. Working out those family issues in therapy can lead the way to a better relationship with your child.

Relationship difficulties. One of the major stresses and adjustments in the postpartum period is maintaining the balance in your relationship with your partner. Babies require you to rethink the way you have set up your relationship: who takes care of whom, who pays the bills, who makes the money, who has veto power. All the discussions you may have had, and all your expectations and fantasies, often dissolve when you bring the new baby home. The most powerful model in the back of your mind for how a family functions is your family when you were growing up. You may be overwhelmed to find yourself suddenly in a younger version of your parents' marriage, acting just as they did and expecting your partner to do the same.

Please don't feel devastated by these changes in your relationship. Be assured that they are completely normal. All couples go through an adjustment period after the birth of a baby. You and your partner need to take it slowly. Realize that you can get back to your previous status if you just don't panic. All the changes that have occurred do not mean that your pre-baby ways of relating are gone for good. They're just lost in the fog for a while. Spend lots of time discussing what you want, how you're feeling, and how you'd like your relationship to be. Stick to wording using "I," not "you." Use concrete examples of behavior you'd like to see. For example, "I like it when you hug me when you come home," is much more positive than, "You never pay attention to me anymore." Remember that you're in this together. This transition is hard on both of you. Solutions will only come if you work together.

If you and your partner have a stormy relationship history, your previous problems will likely be magnified after your baby arrives. For instance, if you feel your partner is always critical, this will likely mushroom into a major issue if you are the least bit insecure about parenting. Expect to have to face these ongoing issues as a couple. Counseling is advisable if you are unable to iron out these differences on your own. Do take your conflicts seriously and seek outside help if you need it. Divorce is not uncommon after the birth of a baby. All the stresses and strains of the adjustment period can be an obstacle to reworking your relationship into a stronger and more positive bond.

Self-esteem, self-doubt, and identity. You may find yourself mourning the loss of your old self now that you are "just somebody's mother." Questioning who you are or your value as a person is a common concern after the birth of a baby. You may have had a strong identity as a working person and felt confident in that role. Now you may place less emphasis on that part of yourself or have given it up (for a while or indefinitely) in order to devote more of your energy to parenting. You may feel lost without the old you. Many new mothers feel less valuable without outside income and periodic performance reviews. Caring for an infant does little to bolster self-esteem with the long hours, tiring physical labor, and lack of feedback involved. Your baby never looks up and says, "Good job, mom!" It's no wonder you may question the whole process, let alone your importance as a part of it. Our society does not put a high premium on parenting. Evidence of this is found everywhere, from the low pay for teachers and childcare workers, to the lack of available training for parents, to the snub you may have experienced at a social gathering when you say that you are "just a mother."

You need a bumper sticker that says, "Motherhood is a proud profession." Raising children to adulthood is an immensely valuable occupation, whether you are home all day or balancing paid work with full-time parenting. You need to recognize your strengths, as a parent and otherwise.

List your strengths on paper and review them every day. List your accomplishments, too, in parenting and in other arenas. If you feel that you have given up everything to devote yourself to your baby, identify a part of your pre-baby self that you would like to revive. Then do it. Have your partner care for the baby so you can take a class, indulge a hobby, or develop or improve a skill. Don't be afraid to ask for recognition or a pat on the back from those around you, whether family, friends, or work associates. However, most important is how you talk to yourself and value your own achievements, at home and elsewhere. Tell yourself you did a good job. You are doing the best you can do. If you are proud of yourself and speak up about it or even show this in your body language, others will take note and respect you, too. If you have serious doubts about your ability in a certain area, take the plunge to improve yourself. Take a class, do some reading, or just experiment with a new way of doing things. Don't be afraid to make mistakes. You (and your baby) can survive a mistake or two. People who doubt themselves improve fastest when they jump right in and attempt to solve the problem, rather than brooding about it for a long time. Even if they don't solve their problem perfectly the first time, they feel better and stronger for having tackled it.

If you feel insecure about your identity, try to picture yourself as a pie chart. Your specialness lies in your different roles or components: you may be a daughter, mother, wife, teacher, tennis player, dancer, cook. Each piece of the pie is important to making you who you are. When you have a new baby, the mother part may seem to consume most of the pie. Those other pieces are still there, even if they've shrunk to thin wedges. You need to allow yourself time, and find the energy, to develop those other parts of the pie and feel like yourself again. Being your whole self is another important way in which taking care of yourself will allow you to nurture your baby.

Over the year of postpartum adjustment, there is much that you can do on your own to tackle normal issues like those addressed here. Remember that help is out there, if resolving any of these problems on your own seems daunting. There is nothing the matter with you if the incredible stresses of new parenthood overwhelm you—you're just human, making one of the biggest transitions of your life.

7

Unique Needs: Help for Single Mothers, Older Mothers, Adoptive Mothers, and Families with Fertility Issues

The Short Version
(If You're Pressed for Time)

Not every new mother today fits the traditional model for a family which contains a husband, a wife, and a baby. If you are one of the many mothers who is older, or single, or who struggled to get pregnant, or adopted a baby, the stress level in your life may be very high. This chapter offers support and ideas to help you face the unique challenges of your situation.

For new mothers in these categories, expectations may contribute greatly to how you feel now. Perhaps you worked toward this goal of having a baby for a long time. You may have expected that achieving your goal would make everything in your life perfect. Or, if you are a single mother who chose to have a baby on her own, you may feel that you worked against tough odds to have this baby. Now that you have it, you expect everything to go smoothly. If your expectations postpartum are that the worst is over or that you should be completely happy to finally have this baby in your arms, you may be sorely disappointed. Having a new baby is difficult, tiring, and overwhelming at times. If you expect it to be otherwise—or if you expect to have all the answers because you're older, more experienced, wanted it so badly, and so on—you may find yourself feeling like a failure, because things just aren't that way. You need to identify your expectations about motherhood and the myths or beliefs that underlie them, and then sort out the unrealistic expectations from the more reasonable ones.

This job of being a new parent will not be any different because of the way you got here. New babies don't know what their parents have been through up to this point. They still cry, need to eat, dirty their diapers a lot, and ignore your ideas about schedules and organization. You need to throw those ideas out as well. Take things one day at a time, instead of feeling frustrated because things aren't going according to the grand plan you have in your head about what things should be like.

Another issue that mothers in these categories share is the feeling of being all alone. You may not know another new parent who is older, single, or adoptive. You may feel there's a lack of models for how to take on this job. Because new mothers like yourself may be harder to find than the typical new mother in her twenties with a husband in tow, you may need to work harder to find a supportive group of people in the same boat. Making friends and developing a support network of even one or two people is extra critical for you because you don't fit the usual model. You may have to work hard to find war buddies, but the effort will pay off.

The third issue shared by this category of mothers is physical stress and fatigue. Older mothers may find themselves more tired because of their age. Single mothers may suffer more because they may have no one to give them relief from baby tasks. Women who have had fertility troubles may be more at risk for physical and emotional strain by virtue of their hormonal vulnerability. Plus, they may have multiple babies to nurture. Adoptive mothers may think they don't have to worry about fatigue, because they bypassed the physical stress of pregnancy and birth. But they still need to take care of the baby all day and night, which is a strain in itself. What this means for you is that you need to take extra care of yourself. You need to rest more, nap more, exercise, and eat right, just like any other new mother. You can't expect to just keep going nonstop. No one can. Take care of yourself physically, and arrange to take breaks. These measures are critical for all new mothers.

Older Mothers: Issues and Answers

Lifestyle changes. You may feel as if your life has gone from control to chaos. It likely has. To work on tolerating the changes involved, you can:

- Focus on the positive aspects of your situation. What do you love about it?
- Find one area of your life where you have control and focus on this. Recite to yourself, "I am in control of neatness in this one room," or "I can work on getting my body back by exercising," or "I can still feel in charge at work."

Aging parents. You may be part of what is called the "sandwich generation," caring for aging parents as well as young children. Find some other people who are doing what you're doing and talk with them. Structuring your time and delegating work to others (family members, healthcare workers) when you can will also help you handle the load. Don't forget time off for yourself. You can't nurture others if your pitcher is empty.

Women with Fertility Issues or Women Who Have Adopted

Guilt and worth as a woman. You may feel like a failure "as a woman" if you had difficulty having a baby the "natural" way. You need to congratulate yourself for having the strength and determination to bring this baby into your life. Make a list of things you do well as a parent rather than dwelling on how you got to this point. Try not to play "what if," which is common with adoptive parents: "What if she were my biological daughter? Would I understand her cries better?" Thoughts like this only make you unsure of yourself. Support from other mothers in the same situation is critical now.

Single Mothers

Feeling loved and meeting your needs. Even though you have your baby now, you still have adult needs for companionship, for love, and for feeling important. Work to get those needs met from adult sources. Your baby can make you feel loved at times. But it's important not to rely on a child for feeling good about yourself. First of all, children can't be relied upon to let you know you're doing a good job. Secondly, you need to work on meeting the baby's needs, not on the baby meeting yours. Finding ways to feel good about yourself among adults is an important consideration to squeeze into your day.

Mourning your loss of the ideal. You may feel sad because you are not sharing this life stage with a partner, as you probably imagined you would all your life. You may have lots of anger about this. Allow yourself time to cry, to be angry, and to get those feelings out in a safe way away from the baby. Write, punch a pillow, or scream in the shower. Those feelings are real and you need to take care of them.

Although some women facing these special challenges may have a hard road ahead, they rise to these challenges every day. You need to work at taking care of yourself physically and emotionally, at having fun, and getting breaks or help from others. You need to plan your days quite rigorously to include everything important to your care and the baby's. You need to find others who are in the same boat. And you need to pat yourself on the back and recognize all the good things you're doing well.

Exercise:
Two Minutes for Yourself

Take a kitchen timer with you into the bathroom. Set it for two minutes, and then step into the shower. Turn on the water, fast and furiously. As you let the water flow over you, shout out your anger. "I am so mad! I am furious that I feel so rotten!" Keep raging for two full minutes. Let the water wash that anger off you and down the drain. Imagine your words and feelings swirling away with the water.

After the timer rings, finish your shower, but imagine that there's a healing balm in the water. Every place it touches you, it makes you feel stronger, healthier, and more relaxed.

7

Unique Needs: Help for Single Mothers, Older Mothers, Adoptive Mothers, and Families with Fertility Issues

In society today, there no longer seems to be one "right" way to have a baby. For your grandparents' generation, the common pattern was to be married one or two years and then to start a family. Since most people married in their late teens or early twenties, that placed most new parents in their early twenties. This traditional pattern no longer applies, however. Current statistics tell us that more and more older women are having babies. A significant percentage of those women are single parents. According to the *Statistical Handbook on Women in America*, since 1975 birth rates have been rising only in women between the ages of thirty to forty-four. For younger groups of women, birth rates are declining or holding steady. In other words, more and more women are delaying childbirth until they are in their thirties or beyond. U.S. Census data indicate that the percentage of children born to unmarried women rose from about eleven percent of all births in 1970 to nearly thirty-six percent in 2004. Because not every new mother is living out the "two-parents-in-their-twenties" model, this chapter will address some of the unique stresses and needs that are part of the territory of nontraditional lifestyle choices.

Older Mothers

Just how old do you have to be to be considered an older mother? Most women are reluctant to label themselves as "older," and with good reason. The word is burdened with a truckload of negative associations in our culture. For some reason, the medical community applies the label without mercy. Pregnant women over thirty have "geriatric mother" written in their chart in many hospitals across the country! No matter how old you are, this section may be helpful to you if you feel out of step with your peers in terms of childbearing. If most of your friends, relatives, and coworkers have children who are much older than yours, you may find reassurance and helpful suggestions in this chapter.

Issues for Older Mothers

Expectations. The primary hurdle for many new mothers of any age is their expectations. Prospective parents can spin beautiful dreams about being a mom or a dad. It can be quite upsetting when the reality of parenthood doesn't even vaguely resemble that pretty picture in your head. Older mothers may have the greatest expectations of all. They can easily fall prey to the idea that their greater age and experience will give them an edge in this parenting business. You, or others around you, may feel that you will know better how to parent because you have such a wealth of experience on which to draw. So, you need to prove yourself. You may be accustomed to having most things in life go your way. You've probably worked hard to mold your destiny and make it the way you planned, right down to the timing of parenthood. You may, quite logically, expect life to continue in this vein.

These sorts of expectations can create immense confusion and frustration as you discover how impossible they are to realize. You can't control what kind of pregnancy or birth experience you have. You can't order a child made up to your specifications. What sort of flip-flops your hormones are going to do postpartum is a big unknown. You may be asking yourself, "Did I wait too long to have a child?" On bad days, you may wonder if you made the wrong decision to have a baby at all. Of course you feel badly. Nothing has gone according to plan. So much for your glorious expectations!

Physical stress and fatigue. Because you're not twenty years old any more, you may experience greater physical stress and fatigue during pregnancy and the postpartum period. Many mothers note this difference between the way they felt with the first child and the way they feel with the second or third, even if the children are only two or three years apart. It may or may not be reassuring to note that you feel more tired, more worn out by the physical demands of childbearing just because your body is older. In addition, the loss of confidence in yourself, as you face the uncertainties of this new role, can contribute to a sense of being overwhelmed and fatigued.

Lack of role models. Social isolation may be more intense for older mothers. You may be the only person you know who has an infant. Your friends and contemporaries may have teenagers, or at least school-age children. It may be very difficult to find other new mothers your age. As a result, you may be without a social support network. Feeling so alone can worsen your doubt about what you've done to your life by having a baby. Muddling through without another new mother with whom you can compare symptoms, pointers, and problems can leave you feeling very lost. New parenting is always made easier by having a crew of friends who are fighting the same battles.

Aging parents. If you're older than the average new mother, chances are that your parents (or your spouse's parents) are also older than the average new grandparents. This can create problems in two ways. First of all, if the grandparents are older, they may be less able to provide the physical caretaking that is so helpful in the postpartum period. Your mother or mother-in-law may be unable to come and help with the housework, the baby, and your recovery if she is in her seventies rather than in her fifties. She may not be strong enough or patient enough for babysitting or the other tasks which grandparents have traditionally provided in families. The situation will be even more complicated if grandparents are in ill health. You and your partner may find yourselves in the role of caretaker for two generations: your new baby and your aging parents. This can add greater stress to the already tough job of adjusting to parenthood.

Lifestyle changes, from control to chaos. You may be accustomed to a certain amount of control, competence, and independence in your life. You may look at freedom, privacy, and tranquility as inalienable rights. Yet they vanish with a new baby. Babies create an environment in which messiness, chaos, and crisis are the norm. Baby equipment, baby schedules, and baby's needs all wreak havoc on your controlled, calm life. This is reality. The reality goes on for years as babies turn into toddlers and then teenagers. Children have minds of their own, and it is often necessary to compromise your own needs to meet theirs. This can be a very difficult adjustment. If you've made career and financial changes, like choosing to stay home after working most of your adult life, you may pine for your old identity and independence. Remember, these feelings are normal and legitimate although they may take you by surprise.

Self-Care for Older Mothers

Feeling good in the postpartum period begins with your self-care plan, no matter what your age. Make sure you've read chapter two, which covers the basics. There is also good advice in chapters five and six. Special considerations for older mothers are covered below.

Scale down your expectations. Disappointment may be responsible for the lion's share of your negative feelings. You may have set yourself up by expecting too much, too soon. Perhaps you've bought into the idea that because you are older and more experienced, you'll always make smart choices and do a terrific job as a parent. Perhaps you fully expected to step into the role of Supermom, able to breastfeed your baby while negotiating mergers and preparing to host a dinner for eight that evening (after arranging the flowers, doing 180 sit-ups, and cleaning out the garage).

Now that you know a little more about the realities of life postpartum, readjust your expectations. Try this exercise. Divide a piece of paper into three columns. In the first column, make a list of the images you had of yourself in your new role. For each image, think about the myth that may be hovering behind it. For instance, if you saw yourself baking bread and making baby clothes while your baby slept, the underlying myth might be something like: "I'm organized, creative, and capable — I should be able to do it all." After you've identified four or five such images and the myths behind them, write a statement in the third column that gets you off the hook. In the example above, you might write, "Sure I'm organized, creative, and capable — but I'm under extraordinary physical and emotional pressures right now. It's perfectly fine if I just manage to take care of myself and the baby without accomplishing one single thing more!" If it's tough to write a statement like this for yourself, write it as if you were encouraging a close friend to be easier on herself.

Do whatever you can to counteract your expectations for perfection. Everyone makes mistakes, gets exhausted, has bad days and negative feelings, and struggles to feel good as a parent. You're not exempt from the struggle just because you have a certain number of candles on your birthday cake. There's nothing wrong with you for feeling rotten or disappointed or both. Own up to realities, and then take steps to remedy the situation.

Focus on the positive. Putting aside the myths, there really are advantages to being older in this parenting business. You may, in fact, be more mature and better prepared emotionally to focus on someone else's needs. Your priorities in life may be clearer because of your life experience. Your value system has been well defined and you've had time to test it over the years. You have more perspective. You may have a secure idea of who you are and a clear sense that you are capable of competence. Of course, you may lose track of your self-confidence in the war zone of life with a new baby.

To give yourself a boost, take a deep breath and close your eyes. Tell yourself that the competence and self-assurance that you show in other arenas of your life can transfer to your motherhood role. You are learning a new job. As with all new jobs, there's an apprenticeship period during which you learn lots all at once. But you have a good foundation to build on.

You may be more financially secure than you were ten years ago. This may mean that you'll have fewer money worries than you would have had if you had become a parent then. Perhaps you're able to pay for some of the services that can make such a difference during this transition time, such as babysitting, housecleaning help, and meal delivery. Take advantage of all the hard work you've done in previous years by letting yourself reap the benefits of these sources of paid support, if at all possible.

Develop a support network. If you feel as if you're the only mother ever to embark on this new baby adventure at such an advanced age, you definitely need to find a new parent group consisting of other older mothers. This may seem daunting if there's no one who meets the description in your immediate circle of acquaintances. Take solace in the statistics. If more and more older women are having babies (and they are), there must be others like you out there somewhere.

Start asking around. Talk to your childbirth educator, your minister or rabbi, your child's pediatrician, your obstetrician, your local mental health association, or parenting center. Keep your eyes open wherever there are moms and babies. Be prepared to seize the opportunity to start up a conversation. Carry cards with you that list your name and telephone number. Always keep a pen handy. Talk to every person you know. Someone is bound to have a sister-in-law, cousin, neighbor, or friend who's in the same boat. Then make an effort to get together with even one other older mother on a regular basis. It's wonderful what two people can give to each other. Simply feeling that you are not alone can brighten your day. Be ready to make the first move, for that is an important step in the business of self-care.

Remember the couple. For older parents who may have lived together as a childless couple for years, it can be very painful to make the adjustment from exclusive focus on each other to almost no time together. Making your relationship a continuing priority is of premier importance to creating a happy family. You and your partner need to find ways to remind yourselves that your relationship matters. The easiest way to do this is to schedule "couple time" into your day. Set aside ten minutes at nine p.m. to ask about each other's day. Arrange for a weekly date, when you get out together without the baby. This need not be elaborate. Coffee or a walk in the park can work as well as a dinner-movie-dancing affair. The important thing is that you are saying to each other, "We are important, too." And you are saying that with actions, not just words.

Women with Fertility Issues

You may have worked for a number of years to finally get to this point with your precious baby in your arms. Many women who have experienced difficulty getting pregnant find a wide gap between the expectations and the reality of a new baby. You really wanted a baby! Your behavior — and finances — for a number of years may have been focused almost exclusively on that goal. If you wanted this so badly, why do you feel so rotten now that you have her? The guilt you experience from these thoughts may be great. "There must really be something the matter with me," you think. There is nothing wrong with you. Expectations, once again, may be the culprit.

The particular expectations that go with desperate hope. After investing so much of your time, emotional energy, and perhaps money in having a baby, it's natural to think that achieving your goal will solve all your problems and make you happy. You finally have what you want. But you still don't feel satisfied. Quite simply, you pictured bringing up a baby as an easy and joyful process. You knew labor would be difficult; you went through lots of training to prepare you. The hard part should be over now, and the fun should be beginning!

Maybe you're bumping nose to nose against the reality that new babies are demanding, exhausting, and time-consuming little critters. The process of caring for and adjusting to a new baby is wearing for anyone. This will be true for you even though you've tried so hard and worked ceaselessly to have a baby. You need to recognize that reality. Even with your heart's desire in your arms and all your dreams realized, your life still isn't going to be perfect.

Many women who've endured the agony of trying for years to get pregnant may have lost perspective about other trials in their lives. You may have thought that achieving this goal would make any other problems seem unimportant. Certainly the stress of fertility treatment and deciding whether to adopt can influence a couple's relationship. Some of that stress may be relieved by finally reaching the goal of having a baby. But it's equally likely that you'll trade the stresses of longing for a baby for the normal stress of adjusting to parenthood together. If you had marital conflict before your fertility struggle was rewarded, that conflict isn't going to just go away. The old myth about babies "fixing marriages" is just not true. You'll still have issues in your marriage to work out if those issues existed before your baby was born.

Guilt and worth as a woman. You may be plagued by guilt about how badly you've felt since the baby arrived. How can you feel so miserable, you ask yourself, when you wanted this baby so intensely? Many women who have experienced fertility problems already have doubts about their basic worth as a woman. Not only did you have a hard time getting pregnant, but now you have negative feelings toward your baby. It's easy to come to the mistaken conclusion that there's something the matter with you as a woman for being anything less than ecstatically happy all the time. "If I were in working order as a woman, I would have been able to get pregnant sooner," you may tell yourself; "I would love every moment of being a mother if I weren't so deficient." The reality of motherhood as a difficult, demanding, exhausting job can get lost in the crossfire of self-doubt and blame.

Increased biochemical risk. Research suggests that women who have had difficulty getting pregnant have higher rates of postpartum adjustment problems. This may indicate greater hormonal influence on these women's moods. In other words, if the hormonal balance in your body was out of whack, short-circuiting fertility, your hormones may have to struggle for balance postpartum. As you know by now, most postpartum adjustment problems are caused at least in part by the biochemical free-for-all that goes on in a woman's body after she has a baby. What you are going through now is not your fault. Because you had trouble getting pregnant, you must allow your body extra time to find its balance and give yourself extra nurturing to weather the process.

Multiple births. Women with fertility issues are more likely to have twins, triplets, or more. Mothers of multiples have a higher incidence of postpartum problems for many reasons. Pregnancy with multiples is often more difficult and medically complicated. Because of this physical stress, these women may be more emotionally depleted and stressed even before giving birth. Prior to pregnancy, they may have experienced numerous fertility treatments with hormonal interventions which send them on emotional roller coasters. Miscarriages and pregnancy loss may add further challenge. These prenatal influences are then topped by the overwhelming demands of more than one infant. Among mothers of multiples, the chance of having postpartum depression may be one in three, although these emotions often do not surface until months after birth, when the stress finally takes its toll.

Relationship stress. Couples who have been through fertility treatment often enter the postpartum period at risk. The relationship may have been taxed by the anxiety of waiting each month to see if pregnancy has been achieved. Sex on demand stresses the spontaneity a couple may cherish. Each partner may silently blame or suspect the other for the couple's infertility, regardless of what the medical experts have deduced about the source of fertility difficulties. Likewise, these couples may already be keeping score about which party has suffered the most, even before the stress of new parenthood hits.

Issues related to adoption. Many parents who adopt are faced with an issue that's peculiar to their situation: little time to prepare emotionally for the arrival of their baby. More and more adoptions are open, with the birth mother even inviting the adoptive parents to pregnancy checkups and into the birthing room. However, many hopeful couples still find that they get a call from the adoption agency at work one day, with the happy news that "tomorrow you can come get this baby." Two days is not adequate time to prepare emotionally. You may not have made physical preparations, such as buying baby gear or setting up a nursery, because you wanted to protect yourself from getting your hopes up. Suddenly, you have too much to do and to decide. You are catapulted into the role of parenting without the usual gradual adjustment process of nine months of pregnancy. This can leave you feeling very unsure of yourself, wondering how in the world you're going to handle it.

A second issue adoptive parents face, which may continue throughout their lives, is the "what if" game. Most adoptive parents question themselves on many levels. "What if the baby were not adopted? Would I still have so many doubts about how to be a parent? Would I still feel so negative, so lost, blue, and exhausted?" You can torment yourself endlessly with this variety of second-guessing. You will always wonder how things might have been if this were your biological child. This question may be particularly strong if the new experience of parenthood seems less rosy than you had anticipated.

Developing a Self-Care Plan

Bring your expectations into line with reality. Just because you worked for this new baby for many years does not mean that your baby will sleep more, cry less, or be easier to understand than if you had become pregnant long ago. You are subject to the same rules as any other new parents. You still cannot do everything perfectly or control anyone but yourself. Caring for a newborn is still demanding, exhausting, and uncertain work. It's perfectly normal to feel tired, grumpy, insecure, and doubtful. To help combat these feelings, you need to make sure your expectations are realistic. Raising this child to adulthood will be a tough job, but you're as well-equipped as any other parent.

Your expectations may especially be a culprit if you have given birth to more than one baby. Even though twins are increasingly common, the special quality of a multiple birth may cause you — and others — to envision a rosy glow surrounding your life with these new babies. It helps to remind yourself that even if the blessings are doubled (or tripled), so is the work.

There's no connection between length of time trying to conceive and quality of parenting. You can read parenting books, learn, reassure yourself, and keep your eyes set on the goal of being a good parent. You are just like any other parent. The way you will get through this adjustment period is to take care of yourself as best you can. Stay focused on the realities of the situation. Don't blame yourself for the difficulties.

Finding support. Knowing other parents who have suffered through fertility treatment, adopted, or had multiple babies, can be particularly healing during this phase of your life. You may have to work to develop your own network if there's no existing one in your area. Organizations such as Resolve, Inc., which provide support to people with fertility problems may offer groups for others like yourself who now have babies. For adoptive parents, adoption agencies may offer groups that may help take you beyond those first days at home with your baby. In the resources section, we list two groups which support families with multiples. You may need to form your own support group. Find several parents in similar situations. Work to meet and talk with them on a regular basis. If the group only meets once a month, meet with individual members for coffee in between. The more you can see how your concerns are shared by others, the better you'll be able to maintain your perspective on your own life. This ultimately will help you to let go of some of your feelings of guilt and self-doubt.

If you have twins or more, you may find eager helpers at every turn. Be assertive with these kind souls. It's important that anyone offering to help do what *you* need and want, not what she thinks would be fun. Baby-holders may be a dime a dozen when what you really need is someone to regularly tackle the laundry or be in charge of stocking your fridge.

A word to adoptive parents. You may think that because you did not endure the physical changes of pregnancy and birth, you do not need special care after your baby comes to live with you. You may believe that your happy excitement will carry you through these exhausting first months. Think again. You need to set the same limits for yourself as any biological parent. You need a rest period each day. You need to sleep when the baby sleeps. After all, you are up with the baby at night, too. You need to limit visitors to certain times and not feel that you must be ready to entertain at any and all hours. You need to let guests serve themselves. Do not expect to be the perfect hostess. You also need to ask for (and accept offers of) help from family and friends. Meals, errand running, and household chores must all still be done. You need to reserve your energy for taking care of the baby and yourself, if at all possible, just as if you were the biological mother. The stress of trying to do it all is just as great for you. So please follow the advice on physical and emotional caretaking outlined in chapters two and five.

Single Mothers

Facing a new baby largely on your own can be an overwhelming task for any woman. It's quite normal for a new mother to feel stressed, fatigued, unsure of herself, and easily moved to tears or anxiety. When she is tackling parenthood without another adult to provide reassurance and respite, the task can seem overwhelming.

All new mothers need nurturing and support. Single mothers may find that they can accomplish all the childcare tasks, but they sorely miss a back-up system to provide breaks, back rubs, and bread-winning. This lack can be a huge drain on a new mother's energy. Essentially, the need for self-care and social support in the postpartum period is both more important and harder to squeeze into a crowded day for the single parent than for a parent with a partner. Exhaustion and feelings of isolation are quite common and understandable in the single mother. You are expected to give, give,

give all day long to your infant, with no built-in mechanism to get your own needs met. How can you give endlessly with no mechanism to replenish yourself?

Expectations can be a big stumbling block for the single parent as well. This is especially true if you chose to get pregnant and raise this baby on your own, rather than if you're single now because of death, divorce, or an unplanned pregnancy. You likely had the same glowing ideals in your head about the lovely, cuddly times you and this baby would share—snuggled on the bed at the end of a tiring, but fulfilling day—as does any new mother. The reality may seem quite ugly and glaring to you by contrast, now that the hard, exhausting work of newborn care has begun. Resentment and anger can surface as you work to meet the baby's needs with no one there to meet your needs in turn. Likewise, you may have particular trouble confessing that things aren't going well. To do so would seem to admit failure.

If you are here not by choice, but by circumstance, you may not connect your emotional turmoil to the birth and your adjustment to parenting. You may see your unhappiness solely as the result of your situation, which may cause you to ignore the special measures for self-care that all new mothers need to follow "to keep their pitchers full."

Unique Aspects of Single Parenting

Social ostracism. Although single parenting is increasingly common, you may still feel self-conscious about not fitting the traditional pattern you see everywhere around you. Social acceptance of single mothers may be rising, but "family values" proponents continue to challenge *any* choices that do not fit the Mama Bear, Papa Bear, and Baby Bear model. As a single mother you'd have to be living on the moon not to be aware of the widespread disapproval that many people in our society feel perfectly comfortable expressing, even as you struggle to parent your baby on your own. Many single parents have resolved this issue in their own lives, but still feel anguish when society scorns or pities them. Single parents worry tremendously about how their single status will influence their child. Loneliness, guilt, frustration, and fear are all understandable emotions for the single mother trying to make it on her own.

Feeling loved and meeting needs. You may have hoped that having this baby to love would relieve some of your feelings of aloneness. It may. But infant companionship is a poor substitute for the adult variety everyone needs. Many single mothers find themselves plagued by fierce protectiveness for their infants. Single mothers may feel overprotective because of their own feelings of being unloved, insecure, and alone.

If you're depending exclusively on this baby and your new family life to relieve your loneliness, you are likely to be disappointed. Confronting the daily reality that you are in this alone may feel like rubbing salt in a wound. You're constantly reminded that this is not what you had envisioned. It may become all too easy to transfer your adult needs for love and affirmation into your relationship with your baby. Focusing intensely on your baby is appropriate for a while and part of the normal bonding process. But it can be especially difficult for a single mother to maintain some balance between her relationships with other adults and her relationship with her child.

It's impossible to love your child too much. But children cannot meet—and should not be asked to meet—their parents' adult needs. Single mothers, like all other parents, must get their adult needs met by other adults.

Mourning your loss of the ideal. Single mothers may find themselves plagued by feelings of sadness or anger at raising a baby alone. This may not be what they ever expected to do. It's common to hope that, when you do have a baby, you will be in a supportive, committed relationship.

It's important to allow yourself time to grieve the loss of this ideal. You're not in the relationship you always imagined. You miss the attention, physical warmth, and sexual intimacy of a committed relationship. You miss having someone to confide in, to share decisions, and to share your pleasure in watching your baby grow and change.

If you're divorced, or separated from the baby's father, or your partner has died, it's critical that you work through your feelings of loss and grief. Whether you're missing a real person or the loss of your ideal, you still need to distinguish the guilt and anger stemming from your situation from your guilt and anger associated with the baby and all the normal stresses of motherhood. Making this distinction will make it easier to find ways to feel better on both counts.

Lack of role models. Even though the number of single mothers is rising, you may not personally know someone who has lived successfully through this tough situation. There are few obvious examples of real women who are coping well with being a single mother. Maybe some movie stars do it, but think of the extraordinary resources at their disposal! It's difficult to study and learn from the ins and outs, the day-to-day trivia of success as a single parent, when you have no one several steps ahead of you to watch.

A lowered standard of living. Many single mothers find themselves faced with a drop in their standard of living. You may choose not to work for a while, to devote yourself to your child. You need to adjust to the decrease in your income, whether you're a single mother by choice or through death or divorce. Considerable stress arises from your position as sole breadwinner facing the increase in expenses that a baby brings. If your finances were tight before, now they may seem even more restrictive.

Self-Care for Single Mothers

Single mothers need to take care of their own needs just as any new mother must. If you are to fill this role all alone, with no one to give you breaks, planning to get your own needs met is of critical importance. You cannot be a bottomless well of giving if you are running on empty yourself. The first step is to give yourself permission to be a human being as well as a parent. You need fun, satisfaction, companionship, entertainment, and rest. Learn that you will be a better parent if you nurture the other parts of yourself while you are nurturing your child.

Adjust your expectations. After giving yourself permission to take care of yourself, you may need to tackle some of your expectations about yourself as a parent. Do you think you can be Supermom? Are you sure you can excel at work, parenting, making your home a nice place to be, and still find time for ballroom dancing lessons, the PTA, and the League of Women Voters? Think again. No one can do it all.

Once again, the important aspect to focus on is being a "perfectly good" parent. All parents make mistakes, and the majority of children still turn out to be responsible, loving human beings. You may need to work on being more realistic and allowing yourself not to do everything perfectly. Leave the toys out on the floor. Decide not to make the bed. Put some energy into different priorities, such as rocking your baby or soaking in the tub yourself. You can even scream at your baby, or yourself, now and then without being a total screw-up of a mom. Separate the action from the person. In other words, you can goof up in one area, one evening, and still be a good person. You can make a mistake with your child and later apologize. Aim for a balance, with mistakes and triumphs adding up to a successful job. Of course, if you feel the mistakes greatly outweigh the successes, you may want to talk about your situation with a professional therapist, especially if you fear you might harm yourself or your child.

You should expect to feel negative at times. You are undertaking a time-consuming, exhausting job, especially as you're doing it on your own. Expect to have trouble keeping your cool at times. Have a plan in place for taking a quick break and replenishing yourself with a distracting activity, such as showering, walking, calling a friend or even punching a pillow. Expect to struggle to grab some time for yourself, but expect to take on that struggle anyway. On the other hand, do not expect that you will be better at any of this than the next mom. Give yourself credit for being a human being. Expect to learn new habits, efficiency tricks, and ways to meet your own needs. Work to find small ways to make yourself feel good. Try to see reading ten pages a day in a novel as positive, a small step in the right direction, rather than focusing on how many more pages you would like to have read.

Focus on the positive. While it may be difficult to see the good side of single parenting when everything is looking bleak, focusing on the positive might reassure you. Single parenting actually has some benefits over traditional parenting. You may have greater control over raising your child the way you think it should be done. You don't have to negotiate every fine detail of parenting philosophy with someone else. You have greater freedom to do things the way you want to do them. No one will tell you that you're always dressing the baby too warmly or that you need to let him do things more on his own. Later on, your child may really enjoy having you to herself on a daily basis. Children are greedy about parental time. You may avoid conflicts about balancing your attention between your child and your partner.

Another benefit of single parenting is that society in general tends to be much less critical if a single mom must leave her child during the day to earn a living. Married mothers must routinely face such criticism. You may also get more help from others because they realize that you have no partner there with you to pitch in. People may view your situation more realistically and sympathetically, while they may romanticize new parenting for married women.

Social support. As for any new parent, establishing contact with others in the same boat can be incredibly affirming. Search for a single parent support group and find a way to attend. If you cannot find a group, talk to everyone you know about their acquaintances who are also parenting alone. Then arrange to get together, let the children play, and share your experiences. You may find a mentor this way, or at least a sympathetic ear. Seeing that others have similar struggles, and are surviving them, can make you feel less alone and less guilty.

As you accept that you can't do it all, it may become easier to build a support system to help you with day-to-day activities. Allow yourself to rely on family, friends, and neighbors who offer to help. If those in your immediate circle do not offer, ask them for help. A relative who might be willing to babysit one evening a week can give you a much-needed respite. If you know other parents (single or not), offer to trade babysitting hours with them. Everyone needs breaks, not just single mothers.

If possible, involve the baby's father and paternal grandparents in childcare responsibilities. Even a newborn can have visitation with another parent if that parent is responsible. If there are unresolved issues that would make this difficult, consider participating in some counseling with the baby's father. You will be parents together all of your child's life, even if you're never planning to live together. If you can communicate amicably, it can only be beneficial to the baby to be involved with both parents.

It's important to involve your child with other men who are caring and responsive. Can your father, a brother, an uncle, cousin, or male friend step in on a regular basis? Enabling your child to grow up with loving adults of both genders, regardless of the relationship, will foster his (or her) feelings of worth and self-esteem. Finding other adults to share, even minimally, in the parenting burden will help you as well.

Grieving and anger. Unless you carefully planned to become a single parent, you may have many unresolved feelings of loss or anger about your situation. You may need to spend some time working on those specific feelings about what went wrong. You may feel disappointment about the elusiveness of the ideal Mama Bear, Papa Bear, and Baby Bear scenario. In either case, you need to allow yourself to pay attention to your feelings. It takes energy to push those feelings down inside you and avoid them. You need to conserve all the energy you have right now. If you can let your feelings out and experience them, you can begin to accept your situation and move on to make the most of it. Single or married, you'll regret it later on if you don't have the most positive experience you can with your baby. Babyhood only lasts for an instant; then, it's gone.

You may need to set aside time each day to cry, write out feelings, or rant and rave in front of the mirror. Write letters and then tear them up. Give yourself permission to feel the way you do. You will likely find that you have more energy for other pursuits when you quit using so much energy to avoid your feelings. If you find that you just can't let go of the negative feelings about your situation and they are coloring your relationship with your baby, it would be wise to talk to a professional therapist.

Make a structured plan. Because the demands on your time are so great, getting everything down in a schedule is necessary. Map out all the tasks you need to do in a week. Pencil in work hours, childcare hours, and time for yourself. In the course of each day, you need some rest time, fun time, and contact with supportive adults. Single parents with outside jobs have reported that it works best to devote all their attention to the baby first thing after work. Sit down and hold the baby, feed or rock the baby, or play peek-a-boo. Spend at least twenty minutes focusing on the baby before you even change your clothes. You will feel less guilt if you know you've made an effort to build the parent-child relationship before you do anything else. Then you can move on to changing your clothes, fixing meals, and finishing the evening chores. Let the baby play in the crib or on the floor while you eat, take five minutes to shower, or refuel yourself in some other way. You not only gain some time for yourself, but your child will begin to develop some independence and the ability to calm or entertain himself. If your baby is fussy, rely on a front-pack or sling as you fix meals, pick up the house, or take your evening stroll.

The important thing is to make sure that you reserve, and *take*, some time for your own needs each day. If you can fit exercise or lunch with friends into your work schedule, this will be helpful. If not, reassure yourself about the need for you to make a schedule that includes time for your own recreation. Some single parents with calm babies find it helpful to use a kitchen timer and to alternate the focus of their attention between the baby and other concerns. Set the timer for twenty minutes and play with the baby. At the end of that interval, set the timer for twenty minutes more and do something for yourself after settling the baby in the swing, crib, or wherever she'll happily stay. Try alternating in this manner throughout the evening. Make sure you are not using all your twenty minute segments to wash dishes, vacuum, or fold laundry. The plan requires a healthy dose of fun and stress-relieving activities.

Important Note: If you find that putting the suggestions here (and in chapters five and six) into practice does not make you feel better, you may need to seek out a professional therapist. This is especially important if you fear that your resentment, anger, hopelessness, or other painful emotions may cause you to harm yourself or the baby. No matter how bad or hopeless your situation seems, you are not alone. Help is out there. Use the resources section at the back of this book for places to call if you need help right away.

8

Postpartum Disorders Defined

The Short Version
(If You're Pressed for Time)

The range of feelings different women may experience after the birth of a baby is much like the spectrum of light in a rainbow: the distinctions between the bands of color are not always clear; one color or category may blend into the next one. We discussed the more normal reactions on this spectrum in chapter four. In this chapter, we look at the less frequent, more troubling clinical conditions that women can experience in the postpartum period.

Postpartum Mood Disorders. The collection of symptoms that affect postpartum mood comprises the next step along the continuum. The new mother may be depressed, suffering from an amplified version of the crying, exhaustion, anger, mood swings, irritability, sleep problems, and self-doubt of the blues or normal adjustment. In the state called mania, the new mother may have excessive energy, little need to sleep, and extreme irritability. In this clinical condition, mood changes last longer than those in normal adjustment. The symptoms are much the same, but feel worse and interfere to a greater extent with getting daily tasks done. If you have many of the symptoms of the blues, and your baby is more than six weeks old, you may fit this category.

Postpartum Anxiety Disorders. Just like with mood disorders, postpartum anxiety conditions involve an exaggeration of the negative feelings a woman may experience in normal adjustment, but anxiety, worry, and panic are the primary symptoms rather than depression. Women with this clinical condition worry a great deal, have scary thoughts which they feel unable to control (a thought pattern called obsessive-compulsive), or have panic attacks with many physical symptoms such as buzzing in the ears, tingling in hands or limbs, shortness of breath, dizziness, or flushed skin. Often these worries and panicky feelings are so troublesome that the new mother has difficulty getting through her day.

Postpartum Thought Disorder. The rarest of the postpartum clinical conditions is a type of psychosis which occurs only once or twice among every 1,000 new mothers. In postpartum thought disorder, the new mother may have any of the problems described in the previous categories. But on top of these feelings and symptoms, she also experiences life-threatening confusion, hallucinations, or delusions that impede her normal functioning. Women with this condition see or hear things that are not there. They believe that what they are experiencing is real rather than illusory; as such, they can pose a great danger to themselves and their baby. Women with these symptoms need immediate medical attention.

We've provided checklists for each category to help you locate your own feelings along the continuum.

Exercise:
Two Minutes for Yourself

Because there is so much uncertainty in life, and especially in having a baby, you may find yourself worrying about many things. From your child's health and development, to fears about kidnappers or earthquakes or fires, to whether your child will want to ride a motorcycle as a teenager, worries can consume you.

Instead of spending your energy on circumstances and situations that are largely beyond your control, reel in your imagination and focus on what you can do to make your child's life as safe, fulfilled, and happy as possible. Answer every worry with a calming thought. This exercise will show you how.

Take a sheet of paper, or a page in a notebook, and divide it into two columns. Label one column *Worried Thoughts* and the other *Calming Thoughts*. Carry this and a pencil or pen with you wherever you go. Whenever a worried thought pops into your head, write it down. If a calming thought occurs to you right away, write this down, too. For instance, if your thought was, "I'll never get organized. Look at this messy house!" your calming response might be, "Houses with infants in them are almost always disorganized. Relax! You can make a list and start to get things done one at a time."

If you can't think of a calming thought to answer one of your worries, try to imagine that you're not you, but a dear, kind, supportive friend. It doesn't matter if that person is real or just a friend you'd like to have. Now look at your unanswered worry again. What would your friend say to soothe you? Close your eyes and listen. Then write down her words in the calming thoughts column.

Worries are a part of motherhood, but they don't have to dominate your life. Spend some time every day reading just the *Calming Thoughts* column of your list. Dwell on those calming thoughts. Rehearse them in your head. Say them out loud. Sing them to your baby. Practice thinking them, breathing slowly and deeply, until they become second nature to you.

8

Postpartum Disorders Defined

Like many young couples starting families, Carol and Paul had done everything in what seemed to be the right order. They finished college before getting married and then launched their careers. They postponed having their first baby until they were settled in their first house. Down payments and student loans behind them, Carol finally felt that she could take time from her career as a teacher to devote to full-time parenting. She and Paul embarked happily on trying to conceive a child, ecstatic that everything in their ideal timetable had gone so well up to this point.

Month after month as Carol got her period, her mood turned from happy to grim. Finally, after eight months, Carol surprised Paul at the door with a positive pregnancy test. They danced, shrieking with glee, and began right away to plan the baby's nursery and to study up on baby care and baby names. The pregnancy went smoothly, ending in a textbook labor and birth. Jenny was a healthy, easy baby, with a head of black tousled hair and blue eyes. Carol and Paul were in love with this sweet little being. Infant care quickly sucked up all their time. Paul stayed home for the first week to trade baby-care duty with Carol. By the time Carol's mother arrived from her home three states away to help with the baby, the family seemed to be settling into a routine.

All Jenny had done during the first week was eat, sleep, burp, and poop. Carol and Paul had enjoyed this first calm week, rocking the baby or gazing into her gorgeous blue eyes. Then Carol was up three nights in a row with Jenny. The baby seemed to have her days and nights turned around, wailing helplessly when Carol laid her down in her crib. Carol's mother offered to take a turn rocking or walking the baby. Carol wanted to do it on her own, despite her fatigue. This was her baby and she wanted to be the first one to bond with her. Carol knew she would feel terribly inadequate if her mother could calm down the baby when she was unable to do so. After those first sleepless nights, Carol broke down and cried uncontrollably five times in two days. Paul and her mother both reassured her that this was probably normal: "Just a touch of the blues." While her mother was there, Carol was able to sneak in an hour's nap each of the next two days and felt somewhat better.

Then came the day when Carol's mom was scheduled to return to her own home. Everything fell apart. Carol was surprised to find herself crying and panicking at the thought of being alone with the baby. She had always considered herself to be a strong person. After all, she had handled thirty thirteen-year-old kids in her classes at school. Why was she feeling so upset? Wasn't this what she had worked toward all these years? Here she was clinging to her mother like a three-year-old left at preschool for the first time! This was the ideal she had been craving: a wonderful baby, a loving husband, and a comfortable home. Yet none of it felt right to her.

When Carol's mother left to catch her plane, she gave Carol a big hug. "You're strong, Carol. You'll find your way," she told her. Carol found her mother's words hard to believe. The next weeks felt chaotic and unsatisfying to her. Everything was a blur of nursing, crying, snatching a few minutes of sleep, and trying to finish just a few baby-oriented household tasks. As Carol became more and more exhausted, she started to worry. Soon she felt absolutely paralyzed by her worries. Would she know how to do the right thing for the baby? Did Jenny want to be fed now? Or did she want to be rocked? Was she sleepy? Did her tummy hurt? The more Carol sought answers in her baby-care books, the more confused she became. She had difficulty returning to sleep after the baby's twice-nightly feedings, sometimes tossing and turning for three hours. She would seem to drift off just as the baby awakened again. When Jenny was five weeks old, Paul came home after his day at work to find Carol sobbing in the midst of piles of unwashed laundry and dirty dishes. He put the baby in her swing, tucked Carol into bed, and rubbed her back until she fell asleep.

At Carol's six-week postpartum checkup, she was obviously tired and withdrawn. Paul came home from work to stay with Jenny, sending Carol out the door for the doctor's office with the warning that she'd better tell the doctor about her mood. Carol's physician did question her about her adjustment to motherhood, and Carol answered mostly in monosyllables, giving only a sketchy picture of her sleeplessness and crying spells. The doctor patted her on the shoulder, explaining that she seemed to be having a rather bad case of the baby blues. He told her to nap when the baby napped and get a sitter so that she could have a night out with Paul. Carol felt somewhat reassured, especially when the doctor told her she'd perk up when the baby began to sleep through the night.

Carol tried the doctor's suggestions for two weeks. Every day when Jenny fell asleep after her noon feeding, Carol lay down on the sofa to try and nap. Unable to relax, she tossed and turned just as she did at night. Paul arranged for the teenager next door to come over one evening so that he and Carol could have dinner at the new Thai place around the corner. They didn't even get past the edamame before Carol insisted they leave. She was too worried about Jenny. She wanted to go home and check on the baby *now*. Every evening after that when Paul came home from work, Carol dissolved into tears. Sometimes, the tears lasted all evening, and sometimes Carol took a shower to calm herself down enough to eat some dinner.

One morning Carol became hysterical as Paul dressed to leave for work. She cried and ranted; she refused to be left alone. Both were surprised by her behavior. This certainly wasn't part of the joyful picture they'd envisioned. Paul called in to the office and took the day off. He phoned every new parent and medical expert he knew. Finally, he discovered a pamphlet on postpartum depression in the childbirth education packet they'd brought home from the hospital. The pamphlet listed the national self-help organization Postpartum Support International.

Paul looked up the web site and signed up for an information packet. He found the name of a knowledgeable local psychologist and the names of other parents he and Carol could contact by phone. Once Carol and Paul connected with these resources and began adopting new strategies, the stress began to ease.

Like Carol and Paul, most new parents don't expect a debilitating emotional reaction following the birth of their child. After all, having a baby is supposed to be one of the most wonderful times in a couple's life. Even when some difficulties are anticipated because of all the changes that accompany childbirth, the reality of postpartum depression is rarely considered. If it's considered at all, most prospective parents say to themselves, "That won't happen to me!" To complicate matters further, emotional reactions following the birth of a baby are often referred to as postpartum depression. You're probably familiar with the term. People use it for anything from constant tearfulness on the part of a new mom to the rarer phenomenon of new mothers who have homicidal thoughts about their baby.

The more professionals have studied postpartum depression, the more they've concluded that it's not a single, distinct entity. Rather, a full range—or spectrum—of emotional conditions and symptoms appears to be possible in the postpartum period. These feelings and complaints most often take one of several definite patterns. This has led to the identification of related but varied emotional syndromes (sets of symptoms) occurring after childbirth. Postpartum depression, postpartum mania, postpartum panic, postpartum obsessive-compulsive disorder, postpartum post-traumatic stress disorder, and postpartum psychosis are the major patterns that we'll discuss in detail in this chapter.

To understand the range of difficulties women experience after the birth of a baby, the idea of a continuum is helpful. This is illustrated in the following spectrum, which first appeared in chapter four. Chapter four delineated how the spectrum begins with the range of normal adjustment, which includes the baby blues, postpartum exhaustion, and the normal emotions of the postpartum period. When symptoms listed under "**Normal Adjustment**" intensify, the new mother may have moved into the range of a clinical postpartum episode, such as depression or obsessive-compulsive disorder. The symptoms may be the same, but they are more powerful, more frequent, and/or more overwhelming. This is especially true if you are not getting up and dressed each day or if you are not caring for your baby's needs.

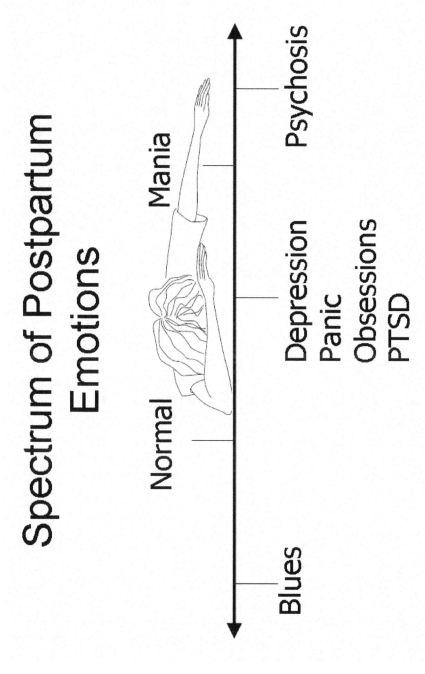

Spectrum of Postpartum Emotions

Many women ask, "How do I know when I have moved from 'normal' to a more serious reaction?" The answer is often a question of good versus bad days, manageable versus overwhelming feelings. If you are having more good days than bad days, you are likely still in the range of normal. If the bad feelings and days greatly overwhelm and outnumber the good feelings and/or the good days, then you have likely moved into the range of a postpartum clinical condition. In such situations, women cannot simply pull themselves up by their bootstraps. The situation needs to be dealt with immediately by a healthcare professional who is knowledgeable about postpartum adjustment. If you think you have a postpartum clinical condition, or you know someone who does, use the resource list at the back of this book to find the best local people who can provide you with an evaluation and treatment plan. Chapter ten offers guidance in selecting a therapist.

Postpartum Mood Disorders

Symptoms and complaints in the postpartum period that primarily involve changes in mood are known as postpartum mood disorders. Postpartum depression and postpartum mania are the major examples of these changes in mood. Research studies have shown that postpartum depression strikes from ten to twenty percent of women with new babies. Figures are not available on the number of women who develop postpartum mania. It's thought that mania may be a warning flag for postpartum psychosis, described later in this chapter. In very rare instances, postpartum depression can also develop into psychosis. Postpartum psychosis only affects one or two in every 1,000 new mothers.

Postpartum Depression
The onset of postpartum depression is sometimes quite fast, within the first two weeks. Just as often, however, its onset is slow and gradual, occurring over a period of eight or more weeks. This clinical condition is characterized by its on-again, off-again nature. A woman will feel great, then miserable, then good, then apathetic, switching from high to low with surprising speed. This condition is distinct from the baby blues, which typically appear full-blown in the first few days after the baby's birth.

Postpartum depression can begin any time during the first two months of your baby's life. The symptoms of depression are variable: if these symptoms persist after your baby is six to eight weeks old and seem to affect you most of the time rather than just some of the time, you have moved beyond normal adjustment symptoms. You may notice extreme changes in appetite—either over- or under-eating. Changes in sleep patterns are also common—sleeping more, or having broken sleep. Other symptoms include tearfulness and crying spells, a short attention span or problems with concentration, and spells of depression. A lack of energy and loss of interest in activities you usually enjoy are also characteristic. As with other hormone-related syndromes like PMS/PMDD, you may find yourself increasingly irritable and overly sensitive.

Women with postpartum depression admit to feeling helpless and hopeless about their situation. They may fear particularly that they cannot be good mothers or will never be able to care for their infants "in the right way." Many a new mother may fear that she has lost her familiar old self completely. She may begin to feel like a burden to her partner, family, and friends, unable to see herself in positive terms.

Faced with nagging self-doubts and negative feelings, a woman can rapidly lose her self-esteem. Many women who previously viewed themselves as competent and successful begin to see themselves in opposite terms, i.e., as unsuccessful and incompetent. Very often this is accompanied by a tremendous sense of guilt about inability to live up to personal and societal expectations of being a good mother. Women often say to themselves, "I just can't do this child any good," or "The baby deserves a better mother than I can ever be." As if this weren't enough, many women find their guilt compounded by worries about the effects of postpartum depression on the baby's development. Suicidal feelings or thoughts about harming the baby can haunt a woman as she struggles with these helpless, hopeless feelings.

There's a good deal of overlap between normal adjustment and postpartum depression. As you read the following case example for postpartum depression, think about your own situation. The checklists and examples in this chapter won't provide you with an exact diagnosis, but they may give you an idea about the diagnostic category that fits you most closely. Based on this, you and people close to you can make a decision about whether or not to seek help from the outside.

A Real Mom's Story: Postpartum Depression

Lydia was a twenty-nine year old mother of a robust baby girl. When the baby was five weeks old, Lydia frequently cried when the baby cried. Helene was what the doctor called a "high-need baby" and cried a lot. There was plenty of opportunity for Lydia to fret. "What is the matter with me?" she wondered. "Babies are supposed to cry, and mothers are supposed to comfort them, not join in." Before Helene's birth, Lydia had worked full-time as a psychologist. When her three-month maternity leave was up she returned to work part-time, working three seven-hour days a week. Lydia knew only one other mother with an infant and that friend worked full-time. There were no other people around on her street on the days when Lydia was at home. To make things worse, all her friends at work were either single or had children in college. She felt lonely and isolated.

The days dragged on. Lydia brightened up when the baby had a few hours when her tummy wasn't hurting; then, she was awake and playful. Nevertheless, once Helene started wailing again, Lydia couldn't stop crying. She felt like a complete failure as a mother because she couldn't seem to do anything to comfort her baby. Every evening Lydia badgered her husband to help find a solution.

Had she made the wrong decision to bottle-feed Helene? Was there even such a thing as colic or was this just a meaningless, catchall term, as some experts said? Had Helene somehow been traumatized during the birth or during Lydia's pregnancy? Had it been a mistake to have a baby at all? She felt as if she were talking the issue to death. Her husband didn't say much when she talked but gave her friendly pats and murmured words of encouragement. Then one evening, at the end of an especially long discussion, Lydia's husband suggested that she really seemed to be overreacting. "We have a babysitter two days a week and someone comes in to clean the house. Can't you just cope, Lydia?" he asked her. "After all, you're a psychologist—you know all about coping!" Lydia just blew up! How could he be so calm, so smug, when her life was in such turmoil? She raged at him: she couldn't come and go as she pleased; she couldn't get a decent night's sleep! Her body didn't feel like her own; she couldn't fit into any of her old clothes. She didn't have a moment she could claim for herself. She was either at work trying to look convincing as someone who could help solve other people's problems or she was at home with a screaming baby who arched her back and wailed when Lydia tried to comfort her.

With some tears, talk, and hugs, Lydia was able to open up to her husband about how her life had changed. Before the baby, her friends and confidantes had been psychologists like herself, childless and carefree. Now these same friends looked bored when she talked about Helene's bouts of colic. More and more friends seemed to become mysteriously busy when Lydia stopped by their desk for a chat. She even overheard one colleague in the restroom say to another, "Poor Lydia! She's completely obsessed with that baby. I can't find anything to say to her." The next day Lydia went online, jiggling Helene in her bouncy seat the whole time, to look up postpartum depression. As she read, Lydia found more and more symptoms that matched her situation. She cried frequently, felt lonely and angry at times, and had even lain awake several nights worrying about her life. She realized that she needed to make some changes. There just didn't seem to be anything she could do about Helene's colic but wait it out, but she needed to find some other people who were in the same boat.

After calling her doctor, the hospital, and her childbirth educator, Lydia discovered a postpartum exercise class. She was able to arrange with Helene's babysitter to cover the extra three hours a week. Lydia enrolled right away. The contact with other new mothers was great, as was the feeling that she was getting her body back.

Through the class, she met another new mother in her neighborhood who also had a high-needs baby, born just a month before Helene. Between the two of them, they managed to discover two other local mothers and formed a play group. By the time Helene was three months old, Lydia felt much more at ease with her life and had some important new friends. She could pick up the phone whenever she needed support and reassurance. Helene's colic had eased off to the point where she only cried one hour a day, giving Lydia the chance to see what a lovely, lovable baby she really had.

Checklist of Symptoms for Depression:

- o Irritability
- o Anxiety and worry
- o Crying/tearfulness
- o Anger
- o Difficulty sleeping (especially returning to sleep)
- o Fatigue, exhaustion
- o Negative, depressed feelings
- o Loss of interest in activities usually enjoyed
- o Rapid mood changes
- o Physical symptoms (i.e., headaches, stomachaches, muscle or backaches)
- o Changes in appetite or eating habits

Important Note: If you think you may be suffering from postpartum depression, you'll find guidelines for feeling better in the chapters on self-help (chapters two, five, and six) and professional treatment (chapter ten). If you feel you have struggled with symptoms that have not been addressed above, carry on with this chapter until your symptoms have been accurately described.

Postpartum Mania

Postpartum mania is likely to appear in the same time period as the blues, in the days immediately following your baby's birth. Postpartum mania is often also diagnosed as bipolar disorder. In postpartum mania, women frequently describe themselves as feeling "speeded up;" they have trouble relaxing or slowing down. They may have a decreased need for sleep. The woman with mania may sleep for only two or three hours a night, without feeling tired. Thinking tends to flow quickly from one topic to another. Listeners may have difficulty following the new mother's logic as she talks. Her speech patterns seem different from usual, with a rapid flow of words.

In mania, a woman may sound or feel under pressure to "get it all said." It sometimes seems like she's thinking faster than she can talk. The speed and excitability of her speech require a lot of energy, both to produce and to follow. Distractibility is common in mania, as are instantaneous mood swings, from excitability to irritability to depression. A woman with mania may seem to be a whirlwind of energy. She might make lots of lists of things to do, or clean house excessively, or undertake any number of difficult projects. However, these activities often turn out to be unproductive, as she jumps around from one task to another, leaving a wake of chaos behind her.

Unlike mania unrelated to childbirth, postpartum mania is often not characterized by an elated or euphoric mood. What is most evident is an increase in irritability or excitability. In the first week or so of postpartum mania, no one may notice an impairment in a new mother's thinking: faulty reasoning, poor judgment, and distorted perceptions may be at a minimum. But postpartum mania can progress to the level of impairment very swiftly. If you're having symptoms like the ones described above, seek treatment by a competent professional immediately.

To evaluate whether your symptoms fit the description of postpartum mania, study the checklist which follows the example below. Mark those symptoms that you've noticed in yourself since your baby was born. We'd encourage you to ask someone close to you for his or her perspective on the situation. It can be difficult to see a situation clearly from inside your own head. The following case example may also be of use to you in determining whether you might be suffering from postpartum mania.

A Real Mom's Story: Postpartum Mania

The early days after the birth of her first daughter were a nightmare for Nancy, a thirty-year-old, stay-at-home mom. Nancy hardly rested at all between her daughter Anna's nursing sessions every three hours, sleeping only a couple of hours a night. Instead of feeling tired, she described herself as "bursting with energy." She rushed around the house trying to get things done, but accomplished little as she flitted from one task to another. She would fold laundry for two minutes, then get out the vacuum cleaner, leaving it in the middle of the hall while she went off to scrub the bathtub. When her husband John came home one night, he found wet laundry on the couch and rice burning in a pot on the stove. Nancy was out in the driveway starting to wash the car. The baby was asleep in her swing.

Nancy made long lists of what she had to do, but didn't seem to have the attention span needed to finish any task. The lists became longer and longer. After a couple of days, John, friends, and other family members noticed that Nancy's conversations weren't making much sense. She couldn't keep her mind on any one topic; she kept tripping over her words in her urgency to get everything said. Nancy was frequently irritable, snapping at her husband for such trivialities as bringing home the wrong brand of milk. He began to dread coming home.

Alarmed by these changes in her behavior, Nancy and John finally consulted a psychiatrist. Nancy was put on Lithium, which meant that she had to wean Anna earlier than she'd planned. Gradually, Nancy's symptoms subsided. There was no discussion at the time of postpartum mania or continuing psychotherapy. For years the couple struggled to understand why Nancy had acted so strangely. Nancy was extremely concerned that something similar might happen if she had another child.

When she became pregnant again, Nancy, fearing the doctor's negative judgment, had to work up her nerve to inform her new OB about her history. John came along for support. After listening quietly and respectfully, the doctor said that Nancy seemed to be suffering from guilt about how crazy she had acted when Anna was born. He suggested that Nancy consult a psychologist who specialized in postpartum difficulties. Nancy had difficulty at first opening up and telling her whole story to the psychologist. She was afraid that her behavior would be held against her and she might be seen as an "unfit" parent. John came along again, at Nancy's request. He had no qualms about revealing all the details. The psychologist was not the least bit shocked but simply set out to educate and reassure Nancy and John. They learned that Nancy had experienced postpartum mania, triggered primarily by hormonal changes following childbirth. Armed with this new understanding, Nancy slowly accepted that her odd behavior hadn't been her fault. She realized with relief that she wasn't a bad mom, as she had labeled herself, but simply a woman who had survived a serious postpartum clinical condition.

Checklist of Symptoms for Mania:

- o   Restlessness, agitation, feeling "speeded up"
- o   Little need for sleep, disrupted sleep
- o   Poor concentration, racing thoughts, distractibility (thoughts jump quickly from topic to topic)
- o   Speech seems very fast, pressured, may trip over words
- o   Emotionally reactive, especially susceptible to anger

o Mood swings, with possible elation, irritability, and/or depression
o Impulsive ideas and/or plans without successful completion or follow-through
o May escalate (gradually or rapidly) into problems in thinking (beliefs which seem real but are not):
  ▪ Paranoia
  ▪ Suicidal ideation
  ▪ Extreme confusion or disorientation
  ▪ Delusions

Important Note: If you feel that your experience matches three or more symptoms in the above checklist, and/or you have a family or personal history of bipolar disorder, please seek immediate medical attention. Women experiencing postpartum mania are most at risk of developing postpartum psychosis, and need a combination of medicine and supportive counseling to get better. If your symptoms have not yet been clearly described, please read the next sections below.

Postpartum Anxiety Disorders

Postpartum depression and mania primarily involve changes in your mood. Postpartum anxiety consists of heightened, recurrent feelings of intense worry and/or panic. The anxiety can be vague and nonspecific, focused on life and the world in general, or the worries can be related to specific events and situations. Fears and anxiety-provoking thoughts about the baby are characteristic. Clinical varieties of postpartum anxiety include postpartum panic, postpartum obsessive-compulsive disorder, and postpartum post-traumatic stress disorder, all of which are described in some detail below.

Recent research has shown that about twenty-eight percent of postpartum women suffer from fairly intense anxiety and worry. In about ten percent of women, this anxiety reaches clinical levels, meaning the symptoms are powerful enough to lead to a clinical diagnosis of anxiety. There is some overlap between the two diagnostic categories of depression and anxiety, with the majority of women displaying symptoms of both depression *and* anxiety. Anxiety symptoms usually appear in the first two to three weeks after the birth of a baby, but may not reach a distressing level until several weeks later. If symptoms are not identified and treated promptly, a woman may become depressed in reaction to her anxious feelings. The typical new mother expects to feel confident and happy after her baby is born. She may wonder if there is something gravely wrong with her for having such painful worries. Self-doubt and guilt over not being able to control the worry can worsen the natural blue feelings — the normal crazy — of the postpartum period. This can throw the new mother into considerable depression as well.

Postpartum Panic

Women with postpartum panic frequently remark that their panic attacks and anxious feelings "come out of the blue." A panic attack is an episode of extreme anxiety in which a person experiences frightening physical symptoms, such as shortness of breath, chest pain or discomfort, choking or smothering sensations, dizziness/faintness, tingling or trembling in limbs/hands/feet, and sweating/flushing.

People suffering a panic attack may fear that they're dying, going crazy, or losing control. A general sense of restlessness, agitation, or irritability may be present. All of these symptoms can occur continuously or off-and-on. If you have panic attacks you may have difficulty identifying a particular event or situation as the trigger. The lack of a provoking incident leaves many women feeling even more helpless and overwhelmed.

It's common for people having a panic attack to believe they're actually having a heart attack and to seek medical attention. When no circulatory problems are found, medical personnel must rule out digestive difficulties (such as heartburn or esophogeal reflux) or systemic illnesses (such as lupus erythematosus). Some postpartum women have panic attacks a few times a week, while others may have attacks almost continuously each day. It's even possible — and quite common — to be awakened from sleep by these symptoms.

No matter how frequently you get panic attacks, it seems that you'll never get used to them. Having a panic attack is a truly agonizing experience. The dreadfulness and intensity of the symptoms can leave you exhausted, vulnerable, and apprehensive about the symptoms returning.

Some women with postpartum panic also have recurrent fears and thoughts about harm coming to their children, other loved ones, or themselves. The new mother may get stuck on these thoughts. Such obsessive fears can make problems with depression or anxiety even worse.

You'll probably recognize whether your symptoms fit the description of postpartum panic. Read through the following example, and then mark the checklist for symptoms you've had since your baby was born.

A Real Mom's Story: Postpartum Panic

Mae was the twenty-four year old mother of a six month old boy. Her symptoms began with the blues. She cried nonstop from the day her son was born. Mae was afraid to take care of the baby. She had little experience with infants. At just under six pounds, the baby looked so tiny and fragile. Mae showed so little confidence handling the baby that her husband George was worried. He called his mother, who agreed to stay with them for several weeks.

George's mother was a matter-of-fact person and took on the task of teaching Mae how to care for her baby in a concrete but gentle manner. By the end of her mother-in-law's three-week stay, Mae felt fairly confident about handling the baby on her own.

George was laid off from his job when baby Eric was only two months old. Mae and George thought they'd combine a much-needed break from parenthood with a long weekend job-hunting trip to a nearby city. George's mom returned to care for the baby.

Mae had some dizziness and nausea before leaving on their trip, but chalked this up to a virus. She wasn't about to sacrifice their weekend for some mild flu symptoms. While stopping at a cousin's house on the way, Mae suddenly felt overcome by the heat, even though the weather was mild. Her face, arms, and chest felt on fire. She was having difficulty getting her breath and felt as if everyone was drifting away from her. George rushed her to the hospital while Mae gasped, "I'm going to die" over and over again. Her blood pressure and EKG were fine. The emergency room physician gave her a prescription for Xanax, an anti-anxiety medication. Mae refused to believe that the intense feelings she'd had were "only anxiety." When she returned home, she was given a thorough battery of tests by her own doctor. This physician hesitantly diagnosed her as having lupus, an inflammation of the connective tissue. The doctor admitted to Mae that the blood tests were inconclusive. He prescribed high blood pressure medication and Mae continued on the Xanax. Her panic attacks continued undiagnosed for several more weeks, with Mae experiencing intense hot flashes, chest pains, and horrible fears that she was dying. Still unenlightened, her doctor gave her nitroglycerine for her chest pains. Mae was devastated, certain that she'd die young, leaving her baby son without a mother.

One day in the doctor's waiting room, Mae discovered an article on panic attacks in a magazine. She realized that her symptoms fit the description perfectly. The stresses of her husband's loss of his job and their separation from the baby during the weekend had triggered the initial panic attack. Mae consulted a psychologist who helped her talk for the first time about her parents' divorce when she was seven, an event which haunted her still. With the psychologist's help, Mae learned techniques for handling the panic attacks without medication and for coping with stress in general.

Checklist of Symptoms for Postpartum Panic:

- o   Extreme anxiety
- o   No specific event seems to be a direct cause of anxiety
- o   Shortness of breath
- o   Chest pains or discomfort
- o   Sensation of choking or smothering
- o   Dizziness
- o   Tingling in hands or feet
- o   Trembling and shaking
- o   Sweating
- o   Faintness
- o   Hot and/or cold flashes
- o   Fear of dying, going crazy, losing control
- o   General restlessness and agitation
- o   Extreme irritability

Important Note: If you feel that your postpartum symptoms have now been clearly described, you can find guidelines for feeling better in the chapters two, five, and six on self-care and survival,

and chapter ten on professional help. If not, continue reading below.

Postpartum Post-Traumatic Stress Disorder

Besides being a mouthful to pronounce, postpartum post-traumatic stress disorder is a clinical condition in which anxiety-related symptoms may occur following childbirth. Perhaps you've heard or read about the syndrome called post-traumatic stress disorder, or PTSD. PTSD has come to the attention of the general public through news stories about soldiers returning to civilian life haunted by a range of painful psychological symptoms, from flashbacks to nightmares in which they relive the trauma of war. Rape victims, victims of other violent assaults, and people victimized by natural disasters such as hurricanes or floods are also subject to PTSD. The syndrome is similar, although not identical, in postpartum women. Research indicates that about seven percent of postpartum women develop a post-traumatic stress disorder.

As you'll recall from the last section, postpartum panic usually has no clear cut triggers that set off a new mother's panic attacks. They just seem to come out of the blue. On the other hand, in postpartum post-traumatic stress, the event that sets off the panic attack tends to be associated with a specific trauma. The trauma can be recent, such as potentially life-threatening complications during labor and delivery, or a trauma from the past. A past trauma can include a violent assault that you suffered as a child or an accident in which you almost died. A new mother exposed to a situation that reminds her of this trauma is vulnerable to panic attacks, especially if she's had previous panic attacks. (This is by no means always the case, however). Women experiencing this panic may fear that they'll die if subjected to the traumatic event a second time. For women who have endured traumatic first births, attending childbirth education classes with their second pregnancy can remind them of the horrible first birth and set off a panic attack. Avoidance of the feared situation may occur; for example, women who fear choking may stop eating solid foods out of fear of re-experiencing the earlier trauma.

Unlike some victims of violence who suffer from PTSD, most postpartum women do not have flashbacks in which they lose their grip on reality and actually believe themselves to be in the traumatic situation again. Nightmares about the trauma are also less common in postpartum post-traumatic stress, although both flashbacks and nightmares are possible. As with postpartum panic, panic attacks or avoidance behaviors may wax and wane. Careful discussion and attention to the events surrounding each attack typically reveal a particular situation that provoked the reaction. This, again, is what differentiates the post-traumatic stress from postpartum panic, in which panic attacks appear to come out of the blue.

Clearly, at this point in the continuum of postpartum clinical conditions, you would be well advised to consult a knowledgeable helping professional about coping strategies and the possible usefulness of medication. To help you assess whether you are suffering from post-traumatic stress, we've designed the checklist that follows this example. Carefully study the list of symptoms, marking those that you've experienced. You may wish to ask your partner, another family member, or a knowledgeable helping professional to go over the checklist with you. Exchanging ideas with someone else often provides a clearer picture of your frame of mind. The case history below may also help you understand the symptoms in the context of a real-life situation.

A Real Mom's Story: Postpartum Post-Traumatic Stress

Patti's pregnancy was smooth and problem-free. Her problems started after twenty-one hours of labor. When the baby's heart rate dropped drastically, the doctor performed an emergency Caesarian section. Patti was emotionally and physically drained after her surgery. She didn't feel well enough to go home after the three days in the hospital covered by her insurance company. Since Patti was someone who always expected a lot of herself, she and the baby went home long before Patti felt recovered. As if this were not enough stress, Patti awakened in a pool of blood at four a.m. the next night. Her husband called a neighbor to stay with the baby while an ambulance rushed Patti to the hospital. The bleeding was so bad that both Patti and her husband feared Patti was going to die.

It turned out that a major artery had been nicked during Patti's C-section. The doctors were able to repair it but Patti was very frightened about leaving the hospital and slept badly after she returned home. Her anxiety didn't escalate into panic attacks until she found herself several hours away from a major medical facility one Saturday, three months postpartum, as she and her husband were taking the baby to visit a relative in a rural, somewhat isolated part of their state. Driving down a bumpy, two-lane country road, through fields and woods, Patti began worrying that she might start bleeding again. What if she couldn't find competent medical help quickly enough? What if she died? They were out in the middle of nowhere. There were no comforting "Hospital-next exit" signs anywhere along the road. There wasn't even consistent cell service! Patti's thoughts intensified into a panic attack, sweeping her up in the terror of her last hospitalization. She felt the same dizzying, breathless anxiety she had felt on the ambulance ride the night she had hemorrhaged.

After this experience, Patti stopped traveling anywhere she judged to be an unsafe distance from a major hospital. Thoughts about the horror she had endured, almost dying, overwhelmed her. She continued to have panic attacks. When Patti returned to work from her maternity leave, she discovered that her job description had been expanded to include travel to remote parts of the state. Her immediate impulse was to quit, but she was afraid of what might happen if she lost her health insurance. She and her husband couldn't manage on one income, especially with the added expense of a baby.

With these challenges facing her, Patti consulted a psychiatrist about her panic attacks. She was fortunate to find one who was knowledgeable and sensitive. Together they explored the pent-up feelings and memories that had plagued her. Eventually, her panic attacks were brought under control.

Checklist of Symptoms for Post-Traumatic Stress Disorder

o Panic attacks in response to specific situations (see panic checklist for symptoms)
o Previous trauma, either recent or long ago
o Sensation of returning to the traumatic event—illusion of actually being there
o Nightmares about the traumatic event
o Emotional numbness—inability to feel anything

Important Note: If you feel that your symptoms have now been correctly described, you can find guidelines for feeling better in the chapter two on self-care, chapters five and six on survival, and chapter ten on professional help. If some of your postpartum

experiences still haven't been covered, continue reading in the sections below.

Postpartum Obsessive-Compulsive Disorder

Postpartum obsessive-compulsive disorder is a clinical condition in which the primary symptom is the recurrence of persistent and disturbing thoughts, ideas, or images. These arise spontaneously, without intentional thought, in the first couple of weeks postpartum. Most commonly, these spontaneous and disturbing ideas center on harming your baby somehow. Prevalent fantasies include hurting the baby with knives, or putting the baby in the microwave oven. Other women have reported imagining suffocating their children, throwing them down stairs, or drowning them. Women who are survivors of childhood sexual abuse may have thoughts or fantasies of molesting their children in similar ways. Loved ones such as an older child, a partner, or a parent may also be the object of these fantasies. The possible harm imagined can include accidental events such as automobile crashes or illnesses such as cancer.

Thoughts of harm that can come to infants are extremely common in mothers who have postpartum depression. Two recent studies have addressed the question of the frequency of these "harming thoughts." One study found that forty-one percent of depressed mothers have these thoughts compared to seven percent of new mothers who are not depressed. The second study showed that even more new mothers—up to fifty-seven percent of those mothers who are depressed—had experienced these scary thoughts about harm coming to newborns. Among women who had these thoughts, ninety-five percent had very violent thoughts. Nonviolent thoughts of harm, for example, might be that the baby could suffocate in a blanket at night or contract a rare disease. Violent thoughts of harm such as stabbing or drowning at the mother's hand were much more frequent, almost to the point of being universal among this group of women.

As new mothers become acutely aware of a baby's vulnerability, thoughts like these may occur to them. Imagining such trauma befalling your baby is a common response to hearing about violence in the world. You may play out these disturbing ideas over and over in your head in an effort to make sense of them. This process may be a way to feel more in control and ultimately better able to protect your child in a dangerous world.

Another clue to the origin of these thoughts may be found in the hormone oxytocin. Oxytocin has a role in inducing labor and appears to turn on mothering behavior in laboratory rats. Rats who have never had pups begin to mother other pups in the cage when injected with oxytocin. An important aspect of mothering behavior is looking for danger in the world. If a mother recognizes danger in her world, she can better protect her child. Research on people diagnosed with obsessive-compulsive disorder (OCD) has shown that these people have an excess of the hormone oxytocin in their cerebral spinal fluid. With this excess oxytocin, OCD sufferers appear to see danger everywhere, leading them to wash their hands until they are raw or check their door locks incessantly. Perhaps this excess of oxytocin is also present in new mothers with postpartum obsessions, leading them to perceive danger in every bath or walk past the kitchen knives.

Obsessive thoughts, nonetheless, may cause a woman a great deal of distress and self-loathing as she repeatedly asks herself, "What is the matter with me for thinking this way?" Unlike women who develop postpartum thought disorder and cannot separate fantasy from reality, women with obsessive-compulsive disorder are quite aware that their thoughts aren't real. They are thoroughly repulsed by the images and rarely experience the urge to act upon them. These women are almost universally highly protective mothers, rigorously checking out safety ratings on car seats and investing in multiple bottles of hand sanitizer.

If you have experienced thoughts about harming your infant, or others close to you, you probably feel terrible about these thoughts. They don't at all reflect your true feelings; you don't want to harm your child. Far from it—your child is the most precious thing to you in the world. You would go to great lengths to protect him/her. In fact, it is this heightened concern about your child's safety that is the likely cause of your obsessions.

A less frequent symptom of postpartum obsessive-compulsive disorder is the performance of ritualistic behaviors to protect yourself from having bad thoughts. Women may hide the knives or avoid the kitchen in an effort to ward off thoughts of harming the baby with knives. Some women may avoid basic care, refusing to bathe their baby out of fear of thoughts about death by drowning.

There are many variations on these types of thoughts and related behaviors; we've only given a small sampling here. But if our descriptions seem to fit with your own experience, take a look at the checklist that follows, and mark those symptoms that sound familiar. Understanding that your thoughts are just thoughts, likely linked directly to hormone levels in your brain, and that you aren't likely to act on them, may enable you to ignore them sufficiently to go on with your day when they arise. Professional treatment, including medication, is needed if you are not able to dismiss these thoughts for what they are—merely ideas in your head. Women with postpartum obsessive-compulsive disorder are always clear that such thoughts are wrong, offensive, and the behavior should be avoided.

The differences between postpartum obsessive-compulsive disorder and postpartum thought disorder or psychosis (described later in this chapter) are:

1) the knowledge that the thoughts are wrong and should not be acted on.
2) the disgust the woman feels in reaction to her thoughts of doing harm.
3) avoidance of triggers for the thoughts (or feared action).
4) the absence of religious ideation (often present in psychosis) in obsessive thoughts.
5) the absence of hallucinations or delusions (hearing or seeing things which others do not see or hear).

Women with postpartum obsessive-compulsive disorder have not been known to carry out their disturbing thoughts, while women with postpartum thought disorder are not repulsed by their thoughts and may actually put them into action.

A Real Mom's Story: Postpartum Obsessive-Compulsive Disorder

Carolyn was a thirty-eight year old mother of a son. Happy to be home from her bank job and caring for her sweet, sleepy baby, she was shocked when she began to have thoughts of hurting him. When the baby was one week old, the idea of putting him in the dishwasher just popped into her head as she loaded the dishes. This was followed by thoughts of putting the baby in the oven. The thoughts then progressed to a vague, "I could kill him."

The thoughts terrified Carolyn. She felt she had turned into a monster. How could a normal person have such thoughts at all? She tried closing her eyes and squeezing her temples to stop the thoughts. She played loud music on the radio all day to drown them out. Neighbors in her apartment complex complained to the manager. When she couldn't play loud music anymore, Carolyn took the baby down to a local construction site, hoping the sound of the machinery would keep the thoughts from coming. Then she found herself fantasizing about losing control of the baby's stroller as it rolled into the jaws of the backhoe.

By the third week Carolyn was so scared that she might act on her thoughts, which she seemed unable to control, that she returned to work before her leave was over. She started volunteering for lots of overtime. That way her husband had to pick the baby up at day care, feed, and bathe him before Carolyn even arrived home. She waited two more weeks before telling her husband about the thoughts, feeling tremendous guilt. She would wake in the middle of the night, her heart racing with fear that the thoughts would overwhelm her and she would be driven to act upon them. Her husband was speechless at her revelation. He just picked up the baby and walked out of the room, leaving Carolyn sitting in a daze. After a couple of minutes, he returned and they talked.

Carolyn's husband encouraged her to consult her OB, who prescribed an anti-anxiety drug. The thoughts lessened, though Carolyn remained worried that she might still act on her thoughts. The OB had not explained why such violent and hateful ideas popped into her head.

Carolyn continued to feel guilty and inadequate. She became depressed and began to call in sick every day, staying at home while the baby was at day care. Her supervisor called one day to check on her, encouraging Carolyn to call her OB again. She did, this time telling him about her feelings of depression, worthlessness, and her trouble getting going in the morning. In consultation with a psychiatrist, Carolyn's doctor prescribed an antidepressant medication. Soon, the thoughts disappeared entirely. Carolyn slowly resumed care of her baby with lots of help and support from her husband.

Checklist of Symptoms for Obsessive-Compulsive Disorder

o   Repetitive, persistent thoughts, ideas, images
o   Thoughts arise "out of the blue"
o   Thoughts of a disturbing or alarming nature
o   Thoughts about harm to your baby or other loved ones
o   Clear understanding that it would be bad and wrong to act on these thoughts
o   Feeling that you can't control having these thoughts
o   Active avoidance of thought triggers

Important Note: If you feel that your total postpartum experience has now been described, you can find guidelines for feeling better in the chapters two, five, and six on self-care and survival, and chapter ten on professional help. If you have symptoms that have not yet been described, please read on.

Postpartum Thought Disorder

Postpartum thought disorder is the term used to describe the extreme reaches of the continuum of postpartum emotional difficulties. As the term implies, a new mother suffering from this clinical condition has difficulties with her thoughts. This is not the mere forgetfulness or spaciness that's so common to postpartum women. Instead, this is a form of temporary psychosis in which the new mother loses touch with reality. Changes in mood may or may not accompany the problems with thinking. Symptoms of postpartum thought problems can range from moderate to severe and can progress quite rapidly. The milder symptoms include extreme distractibility and racing thoughts, as in postpartum mania. Significant confusion, poor judgment, and delusions or hallucinations may also be present. A woman might forget what task she is working on midstream. She might leave the baby unattended in a potentially dangerous situation or completely misjudge the baby's needs. She may think, in a paranoid manner, that friends or family members dislike her when in fact they are being supportive.

Postpartum psychosis is the rarest of the postpartum clinical conditions, with only one or two new mothers in every 1,000 exhibiting psychotic symptoms. The onset of postpartum psychosis usually occurs within the first twenty-four to seventy-two hours after the baby's birth. It can also occur at later times, particularly in conjunction with such physical stresses as abrupt weaning or severe sleep deprivation.

This clinical condition can last several days to several weeks, particularly if left untreated. It may begin with the new mother feeling a great deal of confusion and expressing strange ideas that do not match with reality. It can progress to vivid hallucinations, further confusion, disorientation, and delusions about the baby. Postpartum hallucinations and delusions often have a religious quality. For example, a woman may believe that her baby is evil or targeted by Satan and killing the baby is necessary to save him from damnation. She may believe that her baby is Jesus or hear voices telling her that she's the mother of God. The severity and bizarre nature of these thoughts are part of what differentiates them from the obsessions that characterize postpartum obsessive-compulsive disorder. The latter are related to more commonplace, day-to-day activities. A crucial distinction is that women with postpartum obsessive-compulsive disorder have not been known to act on their thoughts about committing violence against the baby, while women in psychosis might.

Women with other postpartum clinical conditions may have vivid fears and strange fantasies about their infant's health and well being but can differentiate between these fantasies and reality. Women with postpartum psychosis accept their bizarre thoughts and beliefs as perfectly sensible. They may hear, taste, see, smell, and feel things that no one else can perceive. These women can't be talked out of their perceptions because they aren't thinking accurately or correctly. Unable to distinguish fact from fantasy, they may lose their ability to control the impulse to act on a thought, however violent or bizarre.

We've made a checklist of symptoms for postpartum thought disorder, just as we did for the other postpartum syndromes. However, a person in psychosis is beyond the stage where self-diagnosis is useful or even possible. If you're close to someone you suspect may be suffering from a thought disorder, read the checklist and mark those items that you think may apply. Whether or not the diagnosis is an exact fit, it's essential to get professional help right away. The lives of both the baby and the mother may be in danger. Use the resource list at the back of this book to find local agencies and mental health professionals.

A Real Mom's Story: Postpartum Thought Disorder

Elaine liked to do things right. She had an easy pregnancy, a textbook, perfect labor, and good early adjustment to her baby. At thirty-six, she was delighted to become a mother. Her husband was ecstatic with their little daughter. Both grandmothers lived nearby and took turns coming for the day to help out just after the baby was born. Elaine napped and read for two or three hours each afternoon for the first week while one or the other grandmother took over with the baby and cooked dinner.

Elaine felt very confident initially, despite some problems with breastfeeding. By the end of the week, when both grandmothers decided to go back to their own busy lives, baby Amy finally seemed to catch on to nursing. That's when the bottom fell out for Elaine.

She hadn't fully realized how important all the help and support had been to her, always having someone there to take the baby or to give Elaine an encouraging pat on the shoulder. She became depressed on her own. She was so nervous that she couldn't accomplish much during the day. At night she had tremendous difficulty sleeping. After Amy's two-week check-up, the doctor put her on a two-hour, round-the-clock feeding schedule, as the baby still hadn't regained the weight she had lost when nursing had been problematic. Elaine would lie awake watching the clock, afraid of missing a feeding, remembering the pediatrician's disapproving scowls when the baby was weighed.

Elaine's husband had a job that required him to work twelve hours a day. Elaine just couldn't ask him for help when he arrived home looking haggard and exhausted at night. She herself was only sleeping two or three hours a night. She felt anxious and jittery much of the time. Her OB prescribed an antidepressant medication that made it necessary for Elaine to wean Amy long before she had hoped. This was a bitter disappointment after all the hard work of that first week. Elaine became even more of a nervous wreck as her hormones jockeyed for balance again.

Like many babies, Amy fussed and cried every evening for about two hours. Elaine felt that she should know what was wrong, to give Amy what she needed. When the crying persisted, Elaine became increasingly frantic. She felt bad about taking the medication, believing that her recovery ought to be a question of "will." Didn't other women pull themselves up by their bootstraps as they adjusted to a new baby? Elaine's self-esteem was crushed as she replayed this question in her head all day and often all night. She truly felt she could do it, if she just worked hard enough.

When Amy was almost three weeks old, Elaine and her husband had a huge argument about Elaine's inability to adjust and her husband's procrastination about household chores. They called each other names and slammed some doors. Each was certain the situation would improve if the other would just "get it together." They had never had such a big fight. Elaine was terrified that their marriage was over.

After the fight, Elaine couldn't sleep for four days. Her depression and anxiety mushroomed. She began to imagine ways to commit suicide. She felt she would rather die than lose her family to divorce.

After her fourth sleepless night, Elaine lost touch with reality. In a hollow voice she reported to her husband that she had committed suicide, died, and was currently in Hell. She was completely withdrawn. Her husband couldn't get Elaine to look at either him or the baby. She just sat on the bed with her arms wrapped around her shoulders, rocking herself and mumbling. As the day went on, her husband made arrangements to hospitalize her. She became catatonic, unresponsive to anyone and unable to move her body at all.

Elaine entered a psychiatric hospital, was given anti-psychotic medication, and was herself again in five days. She was severely shaken by her experience. She continued outpatient psychotherapy after she was released, to address her perfectionism. She and her husband entered couples' therapy to deal with the marital distress that had triggered their fight.

Checklist of Symptoms for Thought Disorder:

- o Extreme distractibility—lose train of thought or forget what you're doing
- o Thoughts jump from one topic to another
- o Extreme confusion—inability to accomplish simple tasks
- o Poor judgment or decision-making
- o Difficulty seeing or understanding things as others do
- o Inability to distinguish fantasy from reality
- o Hallucinations—see and/or hear what isn't there
- o Delusions—ideas that don't match reality

o   Disorientation—inability to recognize familiar people or places
o   Impulsive actions
o   Sudden, irrational changes in mood
o   Sleep disturbance—inability to sleep or to fall back asleep after waking

Important Note: The occurrence of a postpartum psychosis is potentially life-threatening to both mother and baby and requires prompt and aggressive medical attention. Women who have a personal or family history of manic-depressive/bipolar illness or schizophrenia are significantly at risk for developing postpartum psychosis. These women should be monitored by a mental health professional during pregnancy and following the birth of their baby. They should also be given as much support, household help, and supplemental care as the family resources will allow.

Beyond Diagnosis

All women experience some changes in mood and behavior as part of the normal adjustment to the birth of a baby. Biological changes, including dramatic hormonal adjustments, make it all the more difficult for a woman to achieve emotional balance as she adjusts to being a mother. This process is a major life event and requires reevaluating everything about your social patterns and self-image.

We've described each syndrome as if it exists in some distinct pattern along a continuum. In real life, there is a lot of overlap between each diagnostic category. You may have symptoms of more than one clinical condition, or you may move through the spectrum at different stages of your postpartum adjustment. If you or someone you know is exhibiting the problem behaviors described in this chapter, especially in the following list, thorough evaluation and prompt intervention by a competent healthcare specialist is mandatory. Here is a list of critical signs that should not be ignored during the postpartum period.

Danger Signs in the Postpartum Period:

- Sleep problems that increase, especially problems returning to sleep after waking to feed the baby
- Eating problems — eating too much or unable to eat
- An increase in depression or irritability, especially:
    - Self-deprecating thoughts or self-doubt
    - Increasing discomfort with being a mother
    - Fears for the child, infanticidal fantasies
    - Death wish, suicidal thoughts
- Lack of steps to counteract fatigue (i.e., unable to nap)
- Avoiding people, becoming withdrawn, socially isolated
- Difficulty interacting with the baby
- Panic attacks
- Inability to reason: hallucinations, delusions
- Mania — feeling speeded up, decreased need to sleep, distractible, irritable, excitable, and having pressured speech

9

Fathers/Partners and Other Caregivers

The Short Version
(If You're Pressed for Time)

Chapter nine is intended for fathers/partners. Don't stop reading if you are not a father or partner, however. There is helpful information here for anyone who wants to be more helpful to a new mom.

Now that your child is born, you may find yourself in the midst of many significant changes, both in terms of your emotions and your relationship with your partner. These changes may come as a shock to you as the reality of parenthood sinks in. No matter how involved you were in your partner's pregnancy, you still may have felt like an outsider looking in. You may continue to have these feelings when everyone's attention is focused first on the baby, then on your partner, and maybe, as an afterthought, on you.

The goal of this chapter is to help you sort out whatever feelings you have about all the changes in your life now. Take our word for it—you are important. Your feelings have a major influence on your family's well-being.

Normal Changes of Parenthood

Just as new moms go through tremendous emotional and relationship changes, so do all new parents. You may find yourself experiencing a wide range of emotions, from joy to uncertainty to anger. Even veteran parents will go through these changes because of the physical and emotional demands of having a newborn. You may feel overwhelmed by the challenge of providing for your enlarged family and assuming even more household responsibilities. You may feel left out and resentful of your partner's closeness with your child. At the same time, your life may seem richer now and more fulfilled. All of these feelings are normal.

The Relationship Connection

It's crucial to keep in mind that changes in your partner's moods and behavior affect you, and vice versa. Remember those first few months of pregnancy when your partner's moods changed from one minute to the next? Déjà vu. Between sleep deprivation, your baby's feeding schedule, and all the physical and emotional demands of a newborn, you and your partner may feel exhausted, tense, and dissatisfied with each other. Fortunately, infancy lasts a very short time. In the meantime, hold back and do not add any more responsibilities to those you already have outside your home. Help your partner with her postpartum physical and emotional recovery. Enlist all the assistance with childcare and household responsibilities you can find and afford.

Beyond Normal Adjustment

If your partner is having physical or emotional problems that concern you, consult a healthcare provider. Call your partner's obstetrician or the hospital where she delivered. Symptoms of postpartum depression and anxiety typically appear within the first two to three weeks following childbirth. Unlike the "baby blues," normal emotional changes accompanying childbirth which diminish as time passes, postpartum depression and anxiety get worse as the weeks go by. Postpartum problems are very treatable if you get the right kind of help as soon as possible.

Sometimes, it may take the outside perspective of a relative or friend to clue you into recognizing a postpartum adjustment problem. Be open-minded if your family or friends suggest that your partner needs help. Listen to what they have to say. Let them support you in considering what needs to be done. Be strong enough to admit that there may be a problem. Put your family's welfare before your pride.

Exercise:
Two Minutes for Yourself

Imagine yourself walking down a long corridor, a suitcase in your hand. On the walls of the corridor hang pictures of your family, friends, and others who have been important in your life. As you walk along, reach deep inside your memory and recall the qualities of these individuals that most influenced you. Kindness. Compassion. Respect for your individuality. Persistence. A sense of humor. Toughness. Strength. Stop to look at each picture, and ask yourself, "What qualities did these people have that I want to avoid?" Put only those pictures in your suitcase which you want to keep. Leave the others on the walls. If there are some people you want to remember but you don't want to imitate in your new life as a parent, tear off just part of the picture—a twinkling eye or a strong, gnarled hand—to help you remember them.

If you did not have many positive influences from other people while you were growing up, imagine how you would have liked your relationship with your own parents to have been. Create a scrapbook in your mind of the qualities you wish your parents had. Maybe you wish they had been less strict, or made time to play with you instead of always working. Maybe they're just a part of your life. Put this scrapbook in your suitcase, too. Use these pictures to guide you through your journey of becoming the parent you want to be and to assemble new snapshots of parenthood for your children—ones they will want to keep.

9

Fathers/Partners And Other Caregivers

All parents go through enormous emotional and relationship changes following the birth of their child. If you're a new parent, you know this to be true. The problem is that little has been written about what fathers or partners go through and few people talk about it. Who has asked you lately how you are? Chances are that most of the attention is focused on your partner and your baby. But that doesn't make the changes you're experiencing any less important or painful. After all, your world has been turned upside down, too.

In this chapter, you'll discover how normal it is to feel that your whole life has changed now that you have a baby. This may be especially true for first-time parents, but veteran parents must also adjust to postpartum changes with each new child. We'll explore how your partner's postpartum adjustment may be affecting you. We'll give you some guidelines about what to do if problems occur. The chapter concludes with a discussion of how family and friends can approach you and your partner if they notice difficulties in your postpartum adjustment that you may have overlooked. Sometimes, an outside perspective may be what you need to get things back on track.

Your Baby Is Born

For months, you have stood by and watched while your partner's belly grew bigger with the new life growing inside her. Although you probably felt the baby kick, or saw an ultrasound picture, the reality of having a child may have been difficult to grasp. For men, there is no tangible marker of parenthood until the baby arrives. Then, in a split second, you go from cheering on the sidelines to stepping in as quarterback. What a way to join the game! The team is charging ahead and you aren't certain what play has been called. You may feel excited, confused, or scared. One thing is certain — there's no turning back.

If you were present at your baby's birth, you probably experienced many different feelings. You may have been frightened by your partner's pain. You may have been amazed at all that went on. You may have gotten a little queasy. And yet, when your son or daughter popped out, you most likely felt a joy in your heart unlike any other you have known. You may have been so happy that you started to cry. Feelings of tenderness and caring may have welled up inside you.

All these feelings, whatever you experienced, are normal. So are the feelings of fear and uncertainty that may have set in later as you wondered how you were going to care for this fragile new life. For both men and women, the responsibility of having a child who depends solely on the two of you for his or her survival can be intimidating, to say the least. Don't be alarmed. Over time, you will master this parenthood game. For now, take a deep breath and go slowly.

Just as new mothers go through tremendous postpartum changes, so do male and female partners. Emotional ups and downs are part of normal postpartum adjustment. Remind yourself of this. Some partners even experience physical changes along with the expectant mother during pregnancy, putting on weight around the middle or losing sleep at night while she tosses and turns and hoists herself out of bed every few hours to pee. One man we know pushed so hard during his partner's labor that he developed hemorrhoids!

You may not have given birth, but you are still faced with the daily demands and lifestyle changes that come with a new baby. You're awakened in the middle of the night, even though you have to go to work in the morning. If your partner is staying home to care for the baby, you may be doing double duty around the house when you come home from work with cleaning, cooking, and laundry. You say you feel tired? Of course you do! Unfortunately, men are kept in the dark even more than women about what to expect when parenthood begins.

Many adults have very little or no experience at all with newborn babies. It may come as a shock when you find that your child doesn't even smile at you and may not give even the slightest sign of recognition. And newborns look terrible! Who could ever imagine that such a tiny, limp-looking thing could make such a lot of noise? When you're tired and physically run down, it's easy to feel irritable, unhappy, and frustrated. This is a natural response to what may have been in many ways a nasty surprise. Remember the blissful parenthood you were led to believe awaited you? It's time to face reality.

Begin by cutting yourself some slack as you adjust to these changes. Time-outs are called in all major sports, so why not with parenthood? Think about what absolutely needs to get done. Then let go of the rest. Making certain that you and your partner rest as much as you can may be the major priority. Break household tasks down into smaller chunks. Pat yourself on the back for running one load of laundry or for unloading the dishwasher. Keep expectations about your work outside of the home reasonable. You may want to take some time off if you can. This is particularly helpful in the first two to three weeks, during your partner's early recovery. Depending on the flexibility you have with your job, keep work-related demands to a minimum. Now is not the time to push for that promotion or to reorganize your department. You will have time for these things later. Follow the guidelines for making a survival plan outlined in chapter two of this book.

Many partners ask, "How best can I help?" Research has shown there are three concrete ways in which fathers/partners can help the postpartum mom. New moms seem to thrive when given the kind of help they actually want—not what loved ones think they want. So don't guess—ask. Then follow through. Save time; skip the laundry when what would really make her feel better is the vacuuming. Secondly, do not withdraw emotionally. If you find you are getting overwhelmed with your own feelings, find an outlet. Exercise, talk to a friend, vent in a journal. Rally so you can be there when she needs you again. Finally, give in. Defer to her needs and wishes in this fragile adjustment period, even if they seem outlandish or selfish. Chances are that if you meet her needs for a brief while, she will be quickly able to return the favor. The more she is overwhelmed and running on empty, the less she will have to give—to the baby and to you. The more you can help her replenish herself by providing the kind of help she craves, the sooner she will feel better. While these ideas may run counter to your self-preservation instincts, take a deep breath and give them a try. Then sit back and watch for results.

If you're staying home to care for your baby, be certain to rest as you are able. Follow a healthy diet. Take regular breaks. Try to exercise. Find other parents to talk to who are also staying at home. Parent support groups may be offered through your neighborhood elementary schools or local churches. Attend a childcare class. Get all the help you can from family and friends. Plan a night out for you and your partner once every two or three weeks. Although postpartum changes are unavoidable, there are many things you can do to make them less painful.

The "Odd-Man-Out" Syndrome

As a new father/parent, you may find yourself wondering, "Where do I fit in?" The old saying comes to mind, "Two is company; three's a crowd." With your partner's new relationship with your baby, you may feel like the odd one out. Because you haven't experienced the physical changes of pregnancy and childbirth, your partner has a head start on feeling involved. Socially and biologically, there's a stronger emphasis on the mother-child relationship than on the other parent's role in a child's early life. Family members and friends pay more attention to the new baby and new mother than to you. On television, in magazines, and in advertisements, pictures of moms and their babies appear much more often than pictures of fathers and their babies (although these are gaining in popularity). So, what can you do?

If you're feeling like an outsider looking in, there may be many reasons behind this. Ask yourself how much your feelings of uncertainty or not knowing what to do may be interfering with feeling connected to your newborn. Are you at all afraid of intruding on your partner's relationship with your son or daughter? What is your partner communicating about how involved she wants you to be? Some women become very protective and territorial around a newborn, even excluding the baby's other parent to some extent. What did you learn from your parents about this new role? What did you learn from society about parent-child relationships? What kind of parent do you want to be? Ultimately, this last question is the most important one. Despite what you've learned or thought about parenthood in the past, right now is your opportunity to decide how you want to fulfill that role.

While you're struggling to figure out where you fit in your new family structure, you'll probably be expected to do more than usual to support your family's daily existence. In general, this may mean assuming (or at least helping with) some of the responsibilities at home that your partner used to manage. This can range from cleaning and doing the laundry to bathing the baby and fixing bottles to paying the bills. You're playing many different roles at once, perhaps with little training or experience. If you feel incompetent in any of these chores—and especially if your partner yells at you if you do them wrong—you're bound to feel a little confused and resentful. After all, you're trying, aren't you? You may not like what is happening and may feel angry and frustrated. Life was so much simpler before the baby. You knew who you were and what you had to do. Now you're not sure if you're catching, pitching, or playing the outfield. It's no wonder that you feel a little insecure.

If you already shared household responsibilities with your partner before the baby was born, you'll probably adjust more easily to picking up the slack. This is not to say that it will be easy, even if previously you did all the housework and cooking. There is much more work involved in caring for an infant than in any household without babies. You'll have an advantage if you're already an old hand at running the dishwasher and doing the laundry. You may even be the one staying home with your baby while your partner returns to work. Such arrangements are much less common than the other way around, but they're increasing in frequency and often work very well. Whether or not you're staying home, you're more likely now to see yourself and your partner as equals in parenting if you were equal partners in the household before you had a child. This will give you a head start on becoming an active and involved parent and promoting your family's well-being.

Challenge yourself to create your own picture of parenthood that includes everything you want to be as a parent, a partner, and a person. With each generation, men are becoming more and more involved in their children's lives. The impact of this involvement has been tremendous. Fathers and children are happier and healthier as a result of becoming closer. Also, couples seem to have better relationships when both parents take a more active role in parenting. Remind yourself that parenthood is a process. You don't bring your baby home from the hospital and automatically feel like a parent. This takes time to develop confidence. How comfortably you fit into the role changes as your child grows. No parent is an expert from the start. Plan on making mistakes. Your partner will make mistakes, too. Part of your job as parents is to forgive yourselves and go on.

Just because you don't have breasts that leak milk doesn't mean that you can't be just as nurturing a parent as your baby's mother. Babies need much more than milk to grow and thrive. They need love. They need patience. They need strength. If they have two parents with these qualities, they are very lucky indeed.

Three in the Bed

Nowhere may your baby's presence be felt more strongly than in the bedroom. If you find yourself "sitting on the bench" as you observe your partner and baby's relationship, in the bedroom you may feel as if you're sitting in the upper bleachers.

To begin with, you and your partner may not be sleeping together or going to bed at the same time these days. This may be due to nighttime feedings, the demands of breastfeeding, and scheduling differences as each of you adjusts to your new responsibilities. If you're in bed together some of the time, chances are good that all you're doing is sleeping. Who wouldn't? Your partner may still be sore from her stitches. The fatigue people experience in caring for a newborn is enormous. Just being able to get up in the morning and make it through another day is a mark of success.

It's especially important to understand fatigue as a crucial aspect of your partner's moods and behavior. You may have a long day at work, yet if your partner is staying home initially to care for your child, her day is even longer and often much more exhausting. Imagine spending your entire day feeding, burping, changing, holding, and comforting your newborn. Envision doing this for at least eight hours straight with no breaks. Even when the baby sleeps, you're still on duty. It's not as if you can take fifteen minutes off to walk somewhere and have a cup of coffee. No one comes to relieve you and you have no other adults to talk to you. Plus everywhere you look, there's work to be done. The dishes are unwashed, laundry waits to be folded, and there's nothing in the house for dinner. And look at that kitchen floor!

Whichever of you stays home, almost everything you have to give will go to the baby. During the first few months postpartum, you may have little energy left for yourself or each other. This can be very scary. Well—relax. This phase won't last forever. As time passes, you and your partner will spend less time meeting the baby's physical needs and will have more energy for each other. In the meantime, understanding and patience will go a long way toward keeping your marriage from wilting.

Another factor that may be influencing your partner's relationship with you is her close physical contact with the baby. Especially with newborns, there is a great deal of physical care involved. Most new moms who stay at home spend their days feeding, holding, cuddling, rocking, and carrying their child. Such physical contact builds a sense of emotional closeness and affection. With these needs partially satisfied in her relationship with the baby, your partner may seem more remote in her relationship with you. Even though this is part of the normal bonding process that occurs between moms and babies, it may aggravate your feeling of being the outsider. To make matters worse, your partner may not want as much touching. She needs a break from physical contact after spending all day with the baby. At night, she's very likely to be much more interested in sleep than sex.

Put yourself in her shoes. Imagine you had spent the day with someone clinging to you. How physically affectionate would you feel after that clinging creature finally went to sleep? Think about it.

With these thoughts in mind, let's return to the bedroom to talk about sex—the act that created your baby. You say you don't remember what sex is. When you do, you miss it terribly. Maybe you're ready to resume your physical relationship and your partner isn't. Try to keep in mind how fatigued she is, or how desperately she may need a break from physical closeness. It isn't that she doesn't want you. Many women miss having an active sex life after childbirth as much as their partners do. But the constant demands of a new baby have to come first (at least, they have to for a while). There is no way around this. If you have to wait a few more innings to get off the bench, sit tight. Before you know it, you'll be back in the game. It's even possible that renewed interest and a deeper feeling of commitment may enhance your sex life. It has been known to happen.

Like your partner, you may experience some reluctance about renewing your sexual relationship. With the baby's arrival, you may feel as if there's a stranger in the house. This can put a damper on lovemaking. You may not feel the same sense of privacy as you did before the baby arrived. When you were a couple, you were free to spend your time as you pleased, lovemaking included. Now you practically have to make an appointment to spend time together. No spontaneity. No sense of freedom. You are on your baby's schedule. How can you enjoy lovemaking when your child may wake up at any moment, demanding attention? Some couples swear that their child has a sixth sense about when the parents are about to make love!

Lack of opportunity isn't necessarily the only problem. Many partners feel rather horrified at the changes in the new mom's body postpartum. Maybe your partner suddenly looks more like your (or her) mother than the woman you married. And who wouldn't be taken aback by a completely unexpected spray of breastmilk in the throes of lovemaking? You may feel as if your baby is "emotionally" in bed with you.

Although you may think most often about changes in your sex life, what you may be missing more are the feelings of closeness and affection you and your partner shared. Because your baby consumes so much physical and emotional energy, you may have little left for each other. This can be very unsettling. In response to these changes, you may feel rejected, neglected, unloved, or all of the above. You may grow angry and resentful that your newborn has come between you and your partner. You may feel betrayed and sad over this unexpected loss. You may even question why you wanted to have a child and why you agreed to have a child in the first place! This can be true even if you feel great tenderness and affection as you watch your partner with your baby. Perhaps you feel frustrated over how different your life is now. You long for it to be the way it was. You may wonder when you will feel like a couple again. When will it be your turn? Be patient. That time will come.

In the meantime, make certain that you and your partner spend at least ten to fifteen minutes every day talking together. What you say is relatively unimportant. The idea is that you must let each other know that your relationship still matters. Once you have the energy and the confidence, find a sitter so that you and your partner can go out together every two or three weeks. Don't wait until six months or a year has passed. Many couples start having problems after their first child's birth because they stop talking and spending time together. Yes, time and energy may be scarce. But your relationship is the foundation of your personal and shared emotional well-being. Don' t forget this. Set time aside to listen to each other and to review the feelings you're having about your new life. As often as possible, but especially at times when you're feeling frustrated, hurt, or angry, try to understand your partner's situation and what it feels like. Try to express your feelings in words rather than by acting out or sulking. When your partner criticizes you for your way of dealing with the baby, keep in mind that she's speaking out of a biologically programmed protectiveness for your child. Babies benefit from each parent's different nurturing style, even though it can be painful for the couple as they work on accepting those differences and coming up with compromises.

The most practical and productive approach you can take is to arrange what time you and your partner can share alone together. Equally important is to also find ways to feel close together with your child. Go on walks together, take a dip in a pool together, play "This Little Piggy" with one of you on each foot. Become special to each other even though you have a baby. Work to keep it that way.

The Couple Connection

Remember those first few months of pregnancy, when your partner's mood changed from one minute to the next? You may have felt like a human tennis ball, slammed from one hard surface to another, spun in all sorts of different directions. Now, you're back on the court, and find yourself bounced around even harder and faster. This is partly because of the changes your partner is going through with her postpartum physical and emotional adjustment. It's also because of the changes you're going through with your own postpartum adjustment. Changes in your partner's moods and behavior affect you, and vice versa, complicating the situation even more.

You may claim that your partner's feelings and moods don't affect you—that you can shut them out and go along merrily. In all honesty, is it really humanly possible to do this? No matter how hard you try not to be affected, you'll feel differently depending on whether you're greeted with a warm smile and a hug or a sour and angry stare.

Unfortunately, the enormous demands of a newborn can make even the most naturally cheerful people act and sound like the Wicked Witch of the West. When you feel physically and emotionally drained, it's all too easy to become irritable, angry, and out of sorts.

Since it doesn't make sense to get angry at the baby, you and your partner may direct these feelings at each other. Recent research has shown that many new dads do develop feelings of sadness, frustration, loneliness, and even depression. There is a pretty direct correspondence here. As the new mother grows more anxious, depressed, or irritable, your feelings may head in that direction as well. As she worries about the baby or her lack of feelings toward the baby, you will worry about these things too. Know that your feelings are natural and normal, given the changes in your life. Feelings just *are*. You do not have to feel ashamed or see yourself as a failure if you are feeling this way. You have just as much right, and *need*, to take care of yourself as does your baby's mother. You may need to monitor your own emotional state. Depression and anxiety can happen. Face up to these feelings and get the help you need to prevent the family situation from deteriorating even further. The self-care plan described in chapter two can apply to you, too.

One first-time parent commented, "Every evening when I came back from work, it was a war zone. My partner would assault me at the door with how rough her day had been and how miserable she felt. She would yell at me for being able to get away from all this by going to work. It didn't matter if I'd had a good or bad day. She wouldn't ask and didn't seem to care. All I heard about was how bad her life had become. Sometimes she would break into uncontrollable sobs."

"Then, before I could say anything, she would shove the baby in my arms and walk away. If I mentioned that I was tired and needed a break, she exploded about how selfish and thoughtless I was. She told me that I had no idea what it was like to stay home. She said that I didn't want the responsibility of having a baby, just the fun. After a while, I started staying later at work. I didn't want to come home to her fussing and putting me down. The more I stayed away, the more unhappy she became. But at least when I was gone, I didn't feel so bad."

Although this is an extreme example, some of it may sound familiar to you. The point is that your partner's feelings and actions affect you, and your feelings and actions affect her. In addition, the increased pressures and demands of having a baby may naturally lead to greater conflict because each of you feels more stressed and run down. As personal frustration and unhappiness build, you may blame your partner. In turn, she may respond more negatively to you. Typically, this results in more fighting and disagreements, or more distancing and avoidance of each other. Sometimes, the way couples deal with conflict is to pull further away until there is little or no relationship left. Despite a lack of open fighting, this response can be equally damaging to a marriage or partnership. It is often helpful at this point to remember that this situation is hard on both of you. It is not a contest over who has had the hardest day. It is good to stop and remember, even say out loud to her, "We are in this together—let's squeeze out what moments we can for each other and for alone time."

On the other hand, having a child can deepen the positive feelings that couples share. To see your partner holding your newborn may stir strong feelings of love and tenderness in you. To watch her rocking or soothing your baby may intensify your feelings of caring and compassion. To see each other filled with pride and joy at the new life you've created may bring you closer together. While you watch each other struggle through the changes and trials of parenthood, you may develop a deeper understanding and commitment to each other. This can bring about a stronger realization of your ability to face life's challenges and grow from them. These trials can create greater appreciation for what each of you has to offer personally and what a strong team you can be.

Your Family's Well-Being

Although you can't totally eliminate postpartum stresses, there are actions you can take to improve your postpartum adjustment. The most important is to make yourself and your family your top priority for now. Initially, concentrate on the basics: sleeping enough, eating healthily, exercising, and spending time with your partner and child. This may mean temporarily suspending some of your outside activities. Perhaps you'll bowl once a week instead of twice, or golf every other weekend instead of every Sunday. It may mean attending fewer professional association or club meetings. It may mean accepting fewer new responsibilities at work, if you can avoid them. In one way or another, taking care of yourself and your family will probably require staying home more and going out less. Right now, your immediate family needs you more than outside friends, extended family, business associates, and acquaintances.

Infancy doesn't last long, but it's a critical time in your family's life. Because of the physical and emotional demands involved, neither you nor your partner can afford to get run down. Put your energy into caring for yourselves and your baby. Do what you can to see that each of you sleeps and eats adequately. If one of you requires less sleep than the other, let that partner stay up later with the baby. Alternate nighttime feedings so that each of you gets one solid block of sleep. Sometimes breastfed babies can be supplemented with a bottle at night without disrupting their breastfeeding. If not, do what you can to relieve your partner of other physical responsibilities, like laundry or housework.

Always keep in mind that your partner's physical and emotional recovery will affect your postpartum experience. The better she feels, the better you will feel. Working with your partner, prioritize what tasks at home are most important to complete. First make certain that everyone's basic needs are met. Once this is done, choose one or two small goals for each week. These could be as basic as doing a few loads of laundry or cleaning the bathroom. Keep your expectations modest. Don't expect to spend a whole weekend working in the yard. Suspend any remodeling projects you may have. If you have some extra energy, maybe you and your partner can go out. If you can't go out, stay home and relax together. Talk frequently about how things are going and what each of you can do to help the other.

Besides taking these steps, see that you and your partner get regular breaks from childcare responsibilities. Let family and friends do all they are willing to do. Allowing someone else to fix a meal or hold the baby can provide much needed relief. You might get half an hour to put your feet up, take a nap, or be with your partner. Don't worry that your helpful friends are doing too much. Right now, you and your partner are the ones who need a break. If friends and family haven't volunteered their assistance, don't be shy about asking. They'll say no if they want. In the meantime, speak up for what you need, even if this means letting your helpers know when you need a break from them. Be sure to limit the number of visitors you have during the first few weeks your baby is home. This will aid your recuperation. If you feel awkward telling friends who drop by that this just isn't a good time to visit, keep a ratty t-shirt and pair of old slippers by the door. Slip these on before you answer the door to let your visitors know that they need to come another time, after you've had some sleep.

If you don't have family and friends to rely on, you and your partner need to make a schedule for giving each other "time-outs." See that each of you has two to three hours a week to do whatever each of you wants. This time-out can be taken in one whole block, or in several different half hour periods. This may not seem like much of a break, but it's still enough time to recharge. Although halftime passes quickly, the players still feel more energetic when they return to the field. Use your breaks wisely. Don't run around trying to get things done. You'll regret it when you're back on duty. Instead, put your feet up and read the paper. Watch a program you enjoy on TV or watch a funny video. Go out running or biking. Walk out in the garden and smell the flowers. Let yourself unwind. Indulge yourself by just doing nothing. You've earned a rest.

Determining Whether Your Partner Needs Professional Help

Normal postpartum adjustment presents enough challenges. Between ten and twenty percent of all women experience postpartum depression and anxiety. About one in 1,000 women will experience a postpartum thought disorder or psychosis. Postpartum problems can be very scary, frustrating, and unsettling, especially because they occur at a time in your life when you expect to feel so happy. After all, having a baby is supposed to be joyful, not troubling.

Symptoms of postpartum depression and anxiety typically appear within the first two to three weeks following childbirth. Unlike the baby blues, which are time-limited changes in mood primarily due to the hormone changes of labor and delivery, postpartum depression and anxiety often worsen as the weeks pass.

Postpartum thought disorders tend to occur within the first twenty-four to seventy-two hours following childbirth. If you have any suspicion that your partner has a thought disorder—i.e., if she's not thinking clearly at all, has lost touch with reality, or is "speeded up" (in other words, has postpartum mania)—seek help immediately. Don't put off phoning your partner's doctor or taking her to the emergency room if need be (be sure to line up someone to watch the baby while you're gone). Postpartum thought disorder can actually pose a threat to your partner's life or to that of your baby. Prompt medical assistance is absolutely necessary.

For an explanation of postpartum adjustment problems, from the baby blues to thought disorder, refer to chapters four and eight. Remember, your partner is not to blame for her difficulties, nor are you. Use the information in chapter eight to try to sort out what kind of help the two of you may need. This can be a frustrating, terribly painful time for you. It's easy in this situation to lay the blame at each other's feet. Neither one of you is to blame. Blame your symptoms on hormones. Then get help if you need it, right away. Recommendations about professional help are in chapter ten.

Risk For Postpartum Disorders

As with any other health condition, some women will be more at risk for postpartum clinical conditions than others. Risk refers to the likelihood a person may become ill, either physically or emotionally, due to pre-existing vulnerabilities. For example, men who have high blood pressure and a family history of heart disease are more likely to develop heart disease. Research on pregnancy and postpartum emotional health indicates that women with the following risk factors are most likely to experience postpartum clinical conditions: 1) anxiety and depression during pregnancy; 2) prior postpartum episode of any of the clinical conditions described in chapter eight; 3) personal history of anxiety, depression or other emotional health problem outside of pregnancy or postpartum; 4) lack of social support, particularly due to marital conflict/issues; and 5) overall life stress. If your partner is experiencing problems adjusting to postpartum changes and has one or more of the risk factors described in the this section, we advise you to seek professional help now.

Depression and anxiety during pregnancy. Women with depression and anxiety during pregnancy have a fifty percent chance of developing a postpartum clinical condition. Because this is such a strong predictor, if you are reading this book before your baby is born and your partner is already experiencing symptoms, get help now. If your partner had a prior postpartum episode, consider medication now to decrease her symptoms and prevent postpartum problems. There are medications which can be taken during pregnancy without causing harm to your developing child. If she was on medication before the pregnancy and went off to become pregnant, she may want to restart the same medicine, especially if she is beyond the first trimester. As always, this is something to discuss with your healthcare provider (either OB, midwife, psychiatrist or primary care doctor). You'll want to review the benefits and risks to mother and baby before making a decision. Recent studies have shown that untreated depression, anxiety, or stress during pregnancy can increase risk for pre-term labor and birth, as well as affect the baby's birth weight. Carefully weigh the pros and cons as they apply to the expectant mother's situation, so that you both are comfortable with any choice.

A previous postpartum clinical condition. A past postpartum clinical condition doubles the chance your partner will have another. To diminish risk, have your partner deal with any previous postpartum difficulties that have persisted. If you think she's still having symptoms of depression or anxiety that have lasted since your last baby's birth, seek professional help. Without treatment, she may not be able to fully recover from an earlier postpartum clinical condition. Many women suffer through one or more initial episodes of postpartum depression or anxiety before getting help.

Even if your partner no longer has symptoms, she may need to deal with feelings triggered by an earlier postpartum clinical condition. She may still feel angry, sad, guilty, or disappointed about what happened to her. Despite how much she may have tried to push these negative feelings aside, they may be haunting her. Very often, women with postpartum difficulties feel a deep sense of loss over their postpartum experiences. After all, having a baby is supposed to be one of the happiest times in life. If this turns out not to be true, the disappointment can be tremendous. Working on issues in advance will help prevent further problems later.

If you believe that psychological factors such as perfectionism, issues of control, or low self-esteem have strongly contributed to her postpartum difficulties, support your partner in finding a mental health practitioner to address the issues. Ask your doctor or midwife to suggest someone. Get a referral through a local postpartum support group or the hospital where you plan to deliver. Find out if there is a mental health provider in your community who specializes in treating postpartum clinical conditions. Review chapter ten if you decide to seek professional help. It's critical to decide in advance the role each of your healthcare providers will play if your partner experiences a postpartum clinical condition. The best way to prevent postpartum difficulties from getting out of hand is to take quick and effective action.

Emotional health history. If your partner has a history of depression, anxiety, eating disorder, or sexual, physical, or emotional abuse, she is more at risk for postpartum clinical conditions. Research suggests that this is due to both biological and psychological factors. Children who grow up in homes where one or both parents have/had depression, anxiety, or alcoholism inherit those genetic vulnerabilities. These children also learn poor skills for coping with stress and adjusting to life changes. Likewise, they may have insecure or anxious attachments with one or both parents which can further impair social and emotional development. This is also true for women who come from homes where sexual, physical, and/or emotional abuse occurred.

While the best time to get help is before your baby arrives, if your partner has any of these characteristics, then having a mental health "check-up" is a good idea, particularly if she's currently having symptoms of a postpartum clinical condition (refer to chapter eight). Help her understand that what's happening is not her fault, but that it's in her and your family's best interests to get help with problems quickly because of her pre-existing vulnerability. Speak to her OB-GYN, nurse midwife, or pediatrician about a competent practitioner in your area. Then go with her to the visit to show your support and willingness to do what it takes for her to get better.

Marital distress/conflict. Marital conflict puts women at significant risk for postpartum clinical conditions. If you are embroiled in marital distress, address any problems with your partner as soon as possible. Relationship stress is a primary cause of postpartum difficulties. Make certain that you and your partner work out major differences before your child's birth, if possible. This doesn't mean that you have to agree one hundred percent, but make sure you agree enough to allow you to cooperate as partners and parents. If you don't communicate the way you would like, read a book on couple communication, invest in a DVD or attend a class. Effective communication is critical to your success both as partners and parents. Preserve your relationship by spending time together and don't let other responsibilities interfere with your time. Too many couples drift apart after having children. Research shows that many couples report their trouble began after becoming parents. Review the recommendations already discussed in this chapter, and if you're still having problems, seek professional help.

Overall life stress. The more stressful her life is, the greater your partner's risk for postpartum clinical conditions. If either (or both) of you tend to lead your lives in a stressful way, pressuring yourselves with high expectations and a hectic schedule, do what you can to modify these habits. This can be hard to do when you and your partner are commended at work and/or at home for doing it all. It is essential to stop pushing so hard—and there is no time like right now to begin.

Minimize big life changes as much as possible. Resist the urge to pick up a new project at work or start on home improvements. Don't move, change jobs unless you absolutely must. Focus on caring for your partner, your baby, and yourself. That's enough! Although you can't stop life changes from happening, you and your partner may be better able to cope with them if you have a less stressful lifestyle.

From the Sidelines: Some Gentle Advice for Family and Friends

Because of all the changes you and your partner are experiencing, the two of you may not be in the best position to notice problems if they occur. This is another area in which family and friends can be especially helpful. It's easier to see the whole playing field from the sidelines than as a significant player in the game. Although other family members and close friends may be involved with helping you as you adjust to your life with a new baby, they are still likely to have a different perspective than you and your partner.

If you're a relative or friend who has noticed problems brewing, consider taking the following steps. First, approach the new parents in a direct but gentle way. Let them know that you understand they are doing their best in meeting the many challenges of caring for a newborn. If you are a parent yourself, relate some of the difficulties you have experienced. Let them know that they aren't alone. Help them not to feel like failures. Be specific about the changes or problems you've observed that concern you. It may be easier for them to relate to concrete examples of what you see as problematic. Just saying, "You seem unhappy" or "You seem upset" may not be enough. Ask them what they think about your observations. Try to get both partners to share their reactions and discuss what you've said.

Next, assist the couple in thinking about what may need to change for their situation to improve. Offer to contribute your time and energy as part of the solution, if you can realistically do this. Discuss other resources they might use. For example, if the new mom is getting distressed because she has no relief from childcare, explore which family members and/or friends could come over during the week to lend a hand. Find out the days or hours when a babysitter would be most welcome and offer to contact friends and set up a schedule for the next few weeks. You might be able to arrange for these same well-wishers to deliver a hot meal a few times a week, or even every night for a week or so. If the new parents have the money, you might suggest that they hire people to help out with housework, shopping, cooking, and childcare. If money isn't that abundant, there may be a teenager in the neighborhood who would work after school for a modest wage and help with some of the chores or just watch the baby. Even an hour of help a day can be of tremendous value to a new mother. Be creative in reviewing all the possibilities. Encourage the couple to start with what they think will work best for them. Applaud them for their willingness to look for solutions.

If you think the new parents need professional help, let them know this. Use tact in the way you present them with this idea, but be direct and be honest. Explain your reasoning, noting the problems you've observed.

Be prepared for them to react with some discomfort and even become angry with you. This is a difficult suggestion for almost anyone to hear, probably because "requiring professional help" continues to be associated with "being weak" or "being crazy." Take their response in stride. Don't take it personally or strike back with anger. Remind yourself that you have their best interests at heart, whatever their reaction. Remember that sometimes the truth is a hard pill to swallow, especially when it means admitting that all is not well. Realize that it may take time for them to accept what you've said.

If they do decide to seek professional care, help them find someone who is experienced and competent. Ask other people whom they would recommend. Look for someone who has a proven track record of successfully treating postpartum adjustment clinical conditions. If a person with postpartum expertise is not available in your community, choose the individual who is regarded as the most skilled local provider of general mental health services.

Eileen was a thirty-two year old attorney who was thrilled to be having her first baby. It had taken her three years to get pregnant, with the aid of fertility drugs. Carlo, her husband, vividly recalled how excited they were when her home pregnancy test came out positive. "I couldn't believe, after everything we'd been through, we were going to have a child. I felt so blessed. We spent months buying baby furniture and arranging the nursery. Eileen would sit in the rocking chair and sing to her belly. I kept imagining how it would be to hold my son or daughter in my arms. What a great feeling."

After a prolonged labor and delivery, Eileen came home from the hospital with their baby daughter. Already fatigued and run down, only the excitement of having a new baby seemed to sustain her. Usually upbeat and optimistic, she suddenly felt unhappy and discouraged much of the time. A good friend, Sandy, noticed these changes and decided to speak to her. "I didn't know how she'd take it, but Eileen seemed to be less and less herself. She was withdrawing from her family and friends, and that wasn't at all like her. She sounded down a lot. That shocked me, because I was used to her pulling me out of my moods. I didn't want to see her get any worse. I felt I had to say something."

At first, Eileen was startled. She said that she was tired from taking care of her daughter, and that was what Sandy was picking up on. A month later, when nothing had improved, Eileen thought some more about Sandy's remarks. "I knew there was some truth to what she'd said. I knew I was having problems. That was such a change for me. It was scary. I could handle everything that came my way before. Why not now? I knew other women who'd recently had babies and they were doing okay." Finally, with Carlo's and Sandy's support, Eileen went to see a psychologist. She almost cancelled her first appointment. "I felt so ashamed but I learned it was all right not to be Superwoman, and to make the changes that helped me recover. I know Sandy took a big risk in talking to me. I owe her a lot for that."

Be certain immediately to address situations that may become life-threatening. If the new mom tells you that she's having thoughts about harming herself or her baby, insist that she seek professional help at once. Be willing to accompany her to the healthcare provider's office, or set up the appointment, or both. Make sure her partner knows about these thoughts. Encourage her to speak with her partner if she hasn't already. If she's fearful of her partner's response, ask whether she'd like you or another third party to speak to her partner. As horrible as these thoughts may sound, keep in mind that sweeping them under the rug is much riskier than dealing with them openly.

If the new mom is acting psychotic — if she reports hearing voices, seeing things that aren't there, or seems out of touch with reality in other ways — notify her partner first. Then, see that the couple obtains immediate medical attention. The new mom also needs professional help if her main symptoms include rapid speech, extreme restlessness and irritability, lack of appetite and/or insomnia, and what seems like boundless energy. These are symptoms of mania. Because either of these conditions may rapidly worsen, persist in pushing the couple toward seeking professional help. Both the baby's and the mom's life may be at stake.

With both postpartum psychosis and mania, medication and sometimes hospitalization are routinely required. If necessary, enlist other friends and family members to help get the couple into treatment. Remind yourself that the consequences of their not receiving medical attention may be fatal. So do whatever it takes. They will thank you later. For information about the value of medication and strategies for finding a mental health professional, see the following chapter.

10

Beyond Self-Help: Consulting a Professional

The Short Version
(If You're Pressed for Time)

Although you can accomplish a lot by changing how you take care of yourself in the postpartum period, there are limits to what you may be able to do on your own. At some point, you may feel as if you've exhausted your own resources for helping yourself. You really want someone else to guide you through this rough time. Or perhaps someone important to you, such as your partner or a family member, feels that you need to get professional help. If you reach that point, take heart. You are not a failure. The stresses in your life right now have simply become unmanageable. It takes real courage to admit that you need some outside help, guidance, or support. Be proud of yourself if you have that courage. You are taking the first step.

You need to remember several important points when you embark on your search for a mental health professional. First of all, you are the consumer. You need to trust your ideas about what you need now. If you do not feel comfortable either with a therapist or the therapist's recommendations for your recovery, trust your instincts. You may need to shop around before you find someone who fits your personality and needs. You can find someone you can trust, if you hang in there. Look for a therapist who will be a guide and a partner in your effort to feel better—not an authority figure or someone who in any way will treat you with scorn. You know yourself best. You're the only person on earth who knows whether a particular suggestion or course of treatment feels right to you. Convey this knowledge to any therapist you interview. Expect them to respect your judgment on yourself.

There are three main criteria to look for in selecting a therapist. The first is that any therapist you select should be both caring and understanding. Second, the therapist should have some knowledge and expertise about postpartum adjustment as a life transition. He or she should readily acknowledge that this is a tough time in your life primarily *because* you have a new baby.

The therapist's plan for you should be to work through the symptoms of your postpartum adjustment before you tackle any problems from the past. Take this book with you and share the ideas here with your therapist. Let him or her know if you've found the approach here to be helpful. Be explicit in stating that you would like help in putting your self-care plan into action. Finally, the therapist you ultimately choose should have some standard credentials, such as licensure or registration as a psychologist, social worker, or professional counselor. There are detailed guidelines for judging these criteria in the full-length version of this chapter.

Therapy is not a cure-all. No therapist is a miracle worker. Therapists cannot wave magic wands and suddenly make you feel better. Recovery is hard work and will likely include lots of talking about your feelings, experimenting with doing things differently at home, and maybe even feeling worse before you feel better. You will still need to care for yourself in the ways we've outlined in earlier chapters. Therapy may take only several sessions, or it may take several months or longer. Ask the therapist for a treatment plan that will detail the course of action he or she envisions for your recovery. You should not be at all in the dark about this. You have the right and responsibility to communicate your own ideas about what will and won't work for you. Every treatment plan is subject to modification.

Sometimes psychoactive medication can be an important part of a postpartum treatment plan. Needing medication does not mean that you are weak or crazy or a failure. Rather, medication of this kind is used to correct a chemical imbalance in your body, which is partly responsible for your postpartum clinical condition. This is a temporary measure. It does not mean that you'll be on medication forever. There are antidepressant medications, anti-anxiety medications, antipsychotic medications, sleep medications, hormone treatments, and mood-stabilizing medications. Many postpartum women who are experiencing severe problems are treated with one of these drugs or a combination of several. Some medications work quickly, some take longer. Some may have troublesome side effects, while others do not. In most states, only licensed healthcare professionals such as obstetricians, psychiatrists, family practitioners, certified nurse midwives or nurse practitioners, and physician's assistants (P.A.s) can prescribe medications. If the therapist you choose cannot prescribe medicine, but feels that medication would help you, he or she will have to work in consultation with one of these licensed professionals.

Medication is not always the answer or the appropriate treatment. But in some urgent situations, it is the only choice. You need to know that many medications are compatible with breastfeeding, although there may be some that you can not take safely while continuing to breastfeed. If you do not want to wean your baby so that you can take medications, or you do not feel that medication is the right choice for you, you can tell your therapist that you want to try other interventions first. You are the consumer. There are only a couple of situations (i.e., mania and psychosis) in which medication is absolutely essential for your health and the health of the baby.

Exercise:
Two Minutes for Yourself

Close your eyes. Imagine a TV screen in your head. There's one channel that gives you a blank screen. If the channel shows you negative thoughts and worries, grab that remote control; switch back to the blank screen.

When you can hold the blank screen in your head, try switching to a channel that shows you a positive image of yourself in your role as a new mom. See yourself on the screen, coping with your situation, feeling relaxed and calm, looking in control. Hold that picture in your head. Focus on it. Study it in more detail. This is a video you're watching now. Rewind it; look at it again. Put the controller on "pause." How do you feel about that person on the screen? Do you admire her? Is she doing a great job? That's you you're looking at—give yourself a pat on the back. Then take a few slow deep breaths and return to your day.

10

Beyond Self-Help: Consulting a Professional

Julia had a seven week old baby. For the past four weeks, Julia had been feeling extremely tired, tearful, and tense. On the advice of her physician, she'd been napping twice a day. Her doctor had also recommended an antidepressant, but Julia was breastfeeding. She didn't want to give up nursing. She was extremely cautious about taking medication; she didn't like to take even one aspirin. She really wanted to figure out how to feel better on her own. She had a good group of friends in the neighborhood, mothers with infants and older children, who were taking turns bringing the family meals and providing a shoulder to cry on. Julia's husband was still taking a night feeding every other night to give her a break. For two weeks, she had been taking a brisk walk every afternoon around the nearby park, hoping that exercise would lift her spirits. She had even talked to three different phone volunteers from her state postpartum support network. But as Julia worked to put everyone's suggestions into practice, she found that she felt only minimally better. What more could she do? Where could she turn?

The Limits of Self-Care
Many women and their families find that taking care of themselves physically and emotionally can resolve their symptoms. However, just as many women find that, no matter how well they pamper themselves, they continue to feel worse. With each passing day and week, the anxiety, fatigue, tearfulness, and other symptoms lift briefly, only to settle in again like a fog that blocks all the sunlight. Some of this may be part of the usual "two steps forward, one step back" of the postpartum period. Emotions tend in general to fluctuate wildly. There are limits to what self-care can accomplish in many situations.

A woman may be feeling so badly that she cannot get organized enough to do what she knows would help her feel better. Or, as in Julia's case, she may work very hard at doing all the "right things" and still feel overwhelmed by her symptoms. These limits are simply a reality.

It's important to listen to those who know you well when you're trying to decide whether to seek outside help. It's equally important to trust your own judgment. You know yourself best. When weighing input from your family, friends, and partner, it's best to err on the side of getting help rather than plodding along unsteadily on your own. In other words, if you feel you want to seek professional help, you should do so. By the same token, if someone close to you is greatly concerned and is urging you to consult with a professional even though you want to persevere on your own, it's probably a good idea to take that advice and seek an initial consultation.

Certain aspects of your behavior may be clearer to your loved ones than they are to you. At times — and postpartum recovery is one of those times — you may not be able to see yourself as objectively as those around you can. If you go to a psychologist or psychiatrist at someone else's urging, you can take that person with you. Involving them as much as possible can greatly reduce their anxiety about your state of mind. The helping professional may even be able to give reassurance that you're doing well tackling things on your own. The peace of mind that can come with such reassurances will be well worth the cost of an initial consultation. If it seems that a course of therapy, medication, or both are indicated, then you've wisely put yourself in a position where you can get help without delay.

Here are some general guidelines to help you decide when professional help is your best alternative:

1. You fear that you may harm yourself, the baby, or any other person. **Seek immediate medical attention**.
2. You are experiencing manic or psychotic symptoms (you're not sleeping, have extreme irritability, or are out of touch with reality — hearing voices or seeing things which others don't). **Seek immediate medical attention**.
3. You've worked on this issue on your own as long as you feel you can. You simply feel that you need a different perspective to turn things around.

4. You have repetitive, "stuck" thoughts about harm that could come to you or someone you love.
5. You're unable to sleep for more than three to four hours for several nights in a row or have other significant sleep problems.
6. You have no interest in eating, or eating makes you feel sick to your stomach. As a result, you have eaten little in the past few days or weeks.
7. You are unable to take care of the baby or your own needs (dressing, grooming, eating) because of your symptoms.
8. You've worked hard on a self-care plan for at least ten days and still feel overwhelmed by your symptoms.
9. A significant person in your life believes that it's essential for you to get help.
10. You are having panic attacks or anxiety symptoms that interfere with your daily activities.
11. You are having symptoms (crying, anger, fatigue, or hopelessness, for example) which are preventing you from running your life as you would like.
12. You are at least six weeks postpartum and your symptoms are not lifting, but are staying the same or getting worse.

Elizabeth was a forty-two year old anesthesiologist. After twelve years of marriage, she and her husband Larry made the decision to have a baby. It took sixteen months of aggressive fertility treatment before Elizabeth finally conceived. She was sure she'd be coasting along from that point. In her third trimester, she interviewed nannies in anticipation of returning to her position at the hospital after her three-month leave.

Elizabeth had a relatively easy birth. Her baby boy slept well, nursed well, and left Elizabeth wondering why the new mothers she'd known had complained so. Sure, she was tired. This was nothing compared to the many eighteen hour shifts she worked during her residency. Feeling a little bored at home, and with the nanny ready to start, Elizabeth returned to her busy schedule when the baby was only five weeks old. That was when everything began to crash.

Elizabeth still nursed the baby at night and expressed her milk at work in her office three times a day. Her breasts leaked between pumpings. She was so exhausted when she came home from the hospital that she had little energy left for the baby. When she was at work, she missed him terribly and could think of nothing else. Elizabeth began to feel tortured by guilt. She was acquainted with only one other new mother at the hospital, a technician who was fifteen years her junior. She had little in common with this woman and didn't feel drawn to confide in her. Larry offered reassurance and made arrangements so that Elizabeth could take several hours each Saturday to spend as she wished. But Elizabeth was at a loss; she didn't know what to do with the time. She ended up spending most Saturdays and half of Sunday sleeping. She felt ill but wasn't able to identify any symptoms apart from fatigue.

After three weeks of this, Larry and Elizabeth had a serious discussion about her condition. They decided she should return to the exercise class she'd abandoned during her pregnancy out of fear of miscarrying. She got in touch with a local working mothers group and made a commitment to attend their meetings.

The next week, Elizabeth made an effort to get to the exercise class. But something always popped up that made it impossible to go. She woke up with a stiff neck one morning. Then there was an emergency at work she had to resolve. She wrote the date of the mother's group meeting on the wrong night in her calendar. Accustomed to thinking of herself as organized and competent, Elizabeth felt lost instead.

Finally, after three more disorganized weeks, she broke into tears just before a routine procedure. She was so upset that someone else had to be called in to replace her. She sobbed for two hours in her office and wouldn't let anyone in the door. Finally, the head OR nurse called Larry, who came to take Elizabeth home. Before they left, one of Elizabeth's colleagues from labor and delivery sat down with her and expressed her concern. When she said that Elizabeth looked overwhelmed, Larry chimed in with his own concern. Elizabeth wasn't functioning well either at home or at work. Larry mentioned that she didn't seem to be getting much pleasure at all from the baby after striving all that time to conceive. Elizabeth, normally calm and articulate, could only respond by breaking into tears again. As Larry and the OB continued to talk, and Elizabeth continued to cry, it became clear that she needed more than exercise classes or mommies' groups to lift her out of her depression.

If you decide that seeking outside help is your best option, try not to question your choice. You've shown a great deal of strength in being able to say, "I need someone else's help now." It takes considerable courage to admit this. There's still an outdated societal stigma to mental health problems. We treat problems in our brain chemistry as if we have control over those processes. But the brain, just like every other organ in the body, is not controlled by mere determination. When your brain is chemically out of balance, you can no more will it to level out neurotransmitter function than a diabetic person can tell her pancreas to manufacture insulin. While much can help you feel better, just as maintaining a healthy diet can help manage diabetes, chemical changes like depression often require chemical solutions (i.e., medication).

Some people who don't know any better may consider it a sign of weakness to seek the help of a psychologist or psychiatrist. You may find yourself, or those around you, buying into this view. Yet it's simply a false view. Scientists are making discoveries every day that confirm the connection between our bodies and minds. A biochemical imbalance that triggers depression or mania is nothing more to be ashamed of than a biochemical imbalance that triggers diabetes. It's simply foolish not to get treatment—whether medication, talk therapy, or both—when you need it. If you've done what you can by yourself and still don't feel well, outside input is necessary. You are not a failure. You're simply human and your brain, like every other organ, needs help to get back in balance.

It can help to think about a psychologist or psychiatrist as a health partner, as Ellen McGrath suggests in *When Feeling Bad Is Good*. The person you consult will help you see what's missing and give you tools to fill the holes. You need someone to point you in the right direction now and give you a boost. Even a mental health professional can't simply "fix" you. You'll need to contribute your own hard effort, perseverance, and willingness to feel better. Deciding to find someone to help you is your first move. Now you can look forward to having a skilled partner in your struggle, rather than facing the challenge of feeling better on your own.

The Search for a Professional Therapist

Finding a person whom you can trust to help you through this delicate life transition may seem daunting at first. Where do you go? Who can you ask?

There are many qualified professionals out there. You need to think of yourself as a consumer, worthy of respect. You are doing some of the most important shopping in your life. You want to find a person who is not only competent, but caring as well.

The first criteria you want to use when shopping for a therapist are competence, compassion, and specific experience dealing with hormonal transitions. It's important for the therapist to have an understanding of becoming a parent as a major life transition that's unlike other times in your life. You want a helping professional who can connect in a compassionate and respectful manner. The therapist needs to have knowledge about the sources of your suffering. Without specific experience and/or training in postpartum issues, this caring connection is more difficult for the therapist to achieve.

For help in finding a therapist who is knowledgeable about postpartum issues, you may want to contact Postpartum Support International (PSI) or your state postpartum network. The website for PSI is listed in the resources section of this book. Such organizations can give you names and numbers of therapists, but these therapists have not been screened for ability or credentials. That job will still be up to you.

If you can't find a therapist in your area by contacting PSI, or if your state has no postpartum network, go to other sources for referrals. You may want to begin by asking other healthcare professionals you know if they can make a recommendation. Your OB, internist, clergyperson, or childbirth educator is often familiar with mental health professionals and can give you referrals or ideas about where else to look. Local hospitals, mental health associations, or professional psychological organizations may have referral networks which you can use. Other new mothers or mothers of young children may know of professionals in your community who work with these issues. Many health insurance plans can identify or recommend professionals who participate in their organization. Once you have several names, you can begin to contact these professionals by telephone for further evaluation.

Professional standards are the second group of criteria to consider when looking for a therapist to help you through this difficult time. There are national and state organizations that license or register therapists. Professionals who belong to these organizations must meet certain minimum standards of training and experience. This is still no guarantee of competence. It's important to evaluate any potential therapist in terms of qualifications. Licensure or registration with a governmental body is one place to start. There's a list of these organizations in the resources section of this book as well.

Your first talk with the therapist will probably be by telephone. If you only reach an answering service when you call, you can specify that you'd like to talk to the therapist by phone before making an appointment. It's quite natural to feel awkward when you first talk with a helping professional, whether by phone or in person. First of all, you're calling because you're in pain. Allowing yourself to be this vulnerable may be a new experience for you. You may feel self-conscious or ashamed; you may worry about what the therapist thinks of you. Try to clear these thoughts out of your head and think like a consumer. The therapist is the one who's on the spot right now — not you. You should be polite, of course, but don't hesitate to probe thoroughly into the therapist's experience and credentials. Listen to the tone of his or her answers as well. Do you feel that this is a person you'll be able to trust? Do you feel comfortable with his or her voice and attitude?

Unless you're in an emergency situation, it's important that you take the time to shop wisely. This is, no doubt, a lot of work — just one more way you need to begin the process of taking care of yourself. You wouldn't hire a sitter for your child without talking with him or her first and checking his or her references. Choosing a therapist is just the same. You may want to ask about his or her training, academic degrees, areas of specialization, professional affiliations, and licensure or certification. A good counselor will want you to have this information so that you will feel comfortable. If this feels like too much work to do on your own, ask a family member or friend to help out.

Beyond these basic questions about qualifications, you need to ask therapists about their approaches. Do they have experience (and how much) treating postpartum women? How do they view difficulties in this time? What is their treatment philosophy? Do they try everything else before prescribing medication, or is medication their treatment of choice? You may want to keep shopping around if the therapist replies that depression or anxiety in the postpartum period is just like depression or anxiety at any other time. You may also want to avoid a therapist who does not see the postpartum period as an important life transition. The therapist should be able to give specific answers to your questions about his/her experience with these issues. You may need to keep looking if the therapist seems to think of him/herself as an authority figure or expert whose orders you must obey, rather than as a facilitator or partner in your healthcare. Unless your choices are extremely limited, you can keep looking if a therapist makes you feel uncomfortable in any way.

During your initial conversation, you also need to ask questions about policies and costs. What does a session cost? How long does a session last? What is the cancellation policy? Can you make an appointment right now? Does the therapist offer an initial free consultation? Does the therapist ever include family members or significant others in the sessions? Can you bring the baby with you? What is the payment policy? Will your health insurance plan cover any or all of your visits and medication if it's prescribed? Check with your health plan directly to confirm benefits and verify the portion you must pay. If all of this is too overwhelming for you, pass these instructions on to your partner, loving friend or family member. It's a bit like sending someone else out to buy your groceries. You'd better be specific about what you want or you might wind up with a kitchen full of food you don't like.

Once you have found a therapist who comes highly recommended or who seems to be "speaking your language," you can schedule an initial evaluation or therapy session. You need to remember, at this point as well as throughout the therapy process, that you are in charge. The counseling session is your time. We recommend beginning the session by stating that you are looking for a therapist who will treat you as an equal and see you as a partner. Such a therapist will want to hear your story and will want you to take an active role in the session. Share what you have learned in this book about your difficulties, including any relevant symptom checklists from chapter eight.

Let your therapist know what you have tried, what has worked, and what has not. As you talk, pay attention to how the therapist communicates. Does he or she really seem to be listening? Do you understand his or her responses or is it difficult to get past the jargon? Ask any questions that come up for you. If you are a person who needs time to think, take that time to decide if this therapist works for you. You need not set up a next appointment if you are unsure. Trust your gut instincts. While feeling uncomfortable with a new situation such as therapy may be normal, you need to go elsewhere if you feel unimportant or misunderstood.

Counseling is a process, involving work over a period of time. You won't have all the answers by the end of the first session. You're entitled, when this session is over, to feel that your therapist understands your situation, is empathetic and compassionate, and will be able to guide you in a positive direction. You deserve to have the sense that this person respects you and your personal values.

As professionals and women, we strongly believe that you are the consumer in this process, with all of a consumer's rights and prerogatives. You are paying for these sessions (or are paying for them through your insurance). You have an ultimate right to feel satisfied with the product. Be an educated consumer. Trust your judgment about what you need. Trust our judgment that what women need during postpartum adjustment is a healthcare partner, one who can support and foster your own resources. Even though you're having problems now, you are ultimately in charge of your recovery.

We've spoken to many women who have had negative experiences with therapists who did not understand postpartum issues or failed to see the importance of taking care of the immediate problems at hand. These therapists often only made their patients feel worse. If the therapist you've selected wants to talk primarily about your early childhood, your parents, or your dreams—*and if this doesn't feel right to you*—you are perfectly justified in looking for help elsewhere. It's important to address your immediate concerns, like lack of sleep or panic attacks, before you deal with preexisting issues from your past. This here-and-now approach seems to work best for most hormonal transitions. Solve the daily concerns and get to a more comfortable level of functioning before you worry about deeper concerns.

Therapists are as varied as all other people—some are smart, some are not so smart; some are likable, some are rather horrid. Ten different therapists may have ten different views about what is needed in a particular situation. Shop until you find one you feel you can work with right away. There should be some personal rapport and respect on both sides. Therapists are not always right, but it's essential that you find someone you can trust. You may need to interview several therapists before you find the right fit for you. Investing the time in this process will mean a better outcome in the long run.

The Therapeutic Process

By the end of the initial session, you may have an idea about how this therapist views your situation and what he or she would suggest as a treatment plan. In considering the therapist's outline of the help he or she plans to offer, it's important to place an emphasis on your own goals for your recovery. The treatment plan is open to negotiation between you and the therapist. It's appropriate to speak up right away about what parts of the plan you approve and what you might change. Nothing should be done during the course of your therapy that you don't feel completely comfortable doing. There's enough sense of losing control over one's life during this time without being bullied by your therapist into pursuing a course of treatment that feels wrong to you.

Even if you trust your therapist entirely, a leap of faith is sometimes required if you feel a bit worried about some aspects of the treatment plan. You may feel uncomfortable, for instance, about the idea of taking medication, even though your therapist feels that this would be the best and fastest way for you to recover. Your therapist may suggest a new behavior for you to try. Anything different from your usual habits may make you feel uncomfortable, simply because you haven't tried it before. It's important to sort out such feelings from any doubts you may have about the therapist's outlook or approach to therapy in general. Don't abandon a therapist you trust even if specific suggestions for treatment seem scary to you. You can and should have the opportunity to discuss your doubts and fears until you are fully convinced that a given course is the best one.

Julie was a nineteen year old single mother who lived at home with her mother and younger brother. When her baby was six months old, Julie decided to talk to a therapist about the scary thoughts that had consumed her since her baby was born. Julie had daily worries that her baby might die of cancer. The baby's pediatrician reassured Julie that babies rarely contract any form of cancer. But it seemed that every time Julie opened the newspaper, or listened to the television news, there was some report about devastating childhood illness. The thoughts played over and over again like a broken record in Julie's head: "Emily will get cancer, Emily will get cancer." Her mother advised Julie to stay busy and just "not think about it." So Julie went into a frenzy of housecleaning during her long days at home alone with the baby. But the thoughts wouldn't go away. Julie's grandmother, who lived next door, came over to keep her company, but that didn't help either.

Julie had no contact with Emily's father, who lived in another city, and had not spoken to him for months. She had no friends with children. Her friends from high school seemed so silly to her now. They talked about clothes, and going to clubs, and worried about what silly nineteen year old boys thought of them. Julie felt above all this. She had more important issues on her mind, such as taking good care of her daughter. She hoped to get a job as soon as Emily was ready for preschool and maybe to go back to school herself. Julie's friends just couldn't relate to her concerns about the future or her fears about Emily's health.

Even though Julie's mother was supporting her and the baby and never complained about this, she'd lash out whenever Julie mentioned plans about eventually getting a job or moving away with Emily to the part of town where Julie might be able to enroll at the community college. Julie heard about Postpartum Support International on a daytime television program, went to the website, and got the name of a therapist.

In the initial session, Julie talked about the repetitive and scary thoughts that plagued her. Her idea was to learn more about this kind of thinking and maybe find a way to make it stop. She liked the therapist, who explained that the thoughts were due to biochemical changes in Julie's brain, along with the stress of all the new responsibility she faced now as a parent.

Julie found this information reassuring. The therapist suggested that they plan to work together initially for six sessions. During that time, the therapist would give Julie some specific tools to stop her scary thoughts. She also recommended that Julie contact a local support program for single parents. This could give Julie the opportunity to talk with other young people dealing with parenthood by themselves, and would provide comfort and an exchange of ideas.

Finally, the therapist suggested that Julie might want to take a look at where she was going with her life and plan for her eventual independence from her mother. The stress of fighting with her mother every time she talked about making plans to leave home was probably adding to Julie's postpartum adjustment problems. The therapist wanted to know if Julie could bring her mother along for some family counseling sessions.

This idea completely terrified Julie. She felt that she'd never be able to talk about her plans for independence with her mother. Bringing her to therapy would just make the fighting worse. Julie knew that her mother could be vindictive and mean and could certainly pick on her at home for things Julie said in the safety of the therapist's office. Julie expressed these fears to her therapist, even though she was afraid that the therapist would get mad at her, too, for speaking up. To her surprise, her therapist said that she understood Julie's reluctance. They could postpone that part of the treatment plan until later and evaluate it then.

After several weeks, Julie found that the therapist's techniques for stopping her disaster thoughts about Emily were working. Julie wrote down her thoughts in a notebook when she had them and put the notebook away in her dresser drawer. She also wore a rubber band on her wrist that she snapped every time the obsessive thoughts about Emily's health entered her head. She was actually feeling much better. Whole days went by when she didn't have any scary thoughts at all.

Unfortunately, however, the fighting with her mother was getting worse. Julie found herself talking about that conflict more frequently during her therapy sessions. When her therapist again raised the idea of family sessions, Julie was not as upset this time. Sure, talking with her mother would be difficult and she might snap at Julie once they got home. But her mother seemed to be angry at her much of the time anyway. Julie reasoned that maybe it would help, after all, to get a third party involved. She had come to trust her therapist and felt she could take that leap of faith.

Before Julie invited her mother to attend a session with her, she and the therapist carefully planned her strategy for discussing the independence issue without raising her mother's defenses. They also laid out some ground rules for the sessions. The main rule was that neither Julie nor her mother could bring up the sessions in an angry or otherwise negative way when they were at home. This made Julie feel somewhat protected, especially when her mother agreed to abide by the rules. After a couple of family sessions, Julie and her mother found that talking things out made their life together much smoother. Julie started a first-year college correspondence course to give her a jump-start on her education for when Emily was old enough for Julie to take a full-time course load.

Your therapist should respect your treatment goals and comfort level with moving toward them. Scary ideas can be placed on the back burner for a while. Or you can agree to try things in modified form, or in small doses. Your treatment plan is not cast in stone. It should be flexible, based on your feelings and needs. You may feel most comfortable committing to a small number of sessions at first, such as three or four. You'll know the therapist's working style by then and will have a sense of whether you are getting what you need. Above all, your treatment plan should focus your efforts on the problems that seem biggest to you right now. Remember, you're the consumer here. You're paying for a service. If you're not working on the issues that are most important to you, you have a right to make your wishes known and get your therapy back on track (or switch therapists).

Talk Therapy

You may wonder how counseling actually works. What is it about talking things out that can make you feel better? Maybe you feel as if you've already talked about your postpartum issues until you're blue in the face. What good can more talking do?

There are several differences between talking things out with a friend and talking them out with a mental health professional. First of all, the counselor is trained to get you to look at your issues in new ways and from a broader perspective. A good counselor is a facilitator who will listen without judging or punishing you. The type of counseling we recommend requires you to be an active participant. Your therapist can't "fix" you without your participation any more than your parents could have taught you to ride a bike if you only stood by the sidelines and watched.

Therapy may help you discover a different way to tackle negative thinking patterns, master a new self-care skill, or broaden your expectations of your new role. What you say in your sessions is strictly confidential, within certain legal limits. This means you may be more open and honest than you would be with a friend or family member. (These limits vary from state to state, so discuss this issue with your therapist). Since counseling requires that you look at negative feelings, it can definitely feel painful. It can also be stressful, which may be particularly unappealing to you right now when you have so much stress in your life already. Talk therapy requires self-examination. You may not always like what you see. It can be hard to admit, even to yourself, that you doubt your skills as a parent or your decision to have a baby. Yet having the help and suggestions of a nonjudgmental, supportive expert can give you the optimism you need to move forward. Just believing in your power to make your situation better can give you the strength and determination to persevere.

You're highly unlikely to get all the answers you're looking for in just one counseling session. Therapy takes time. When you've mastered the tools you need to cope and when your life feels manageable again, you'll be ready to end your therapy. Termination is part of the therapeutic process. Mixed feelings are normal. You may worry that no one will ever listen to you so closely and kindly again. You may also be relieved to finally feel so much better and to have achieved the picture of your life you'd envisioned. Ending therapy may feel like graduation. Your therapist will talk with you about how to maintain the changes you've achieved. He or she may help you devise a checklist of warning signs to watch for to enable you to stay on track.

Before you embark on the counseling process, you need to realize that there are limitations to what therapy can do for you. Sometimes people end up feeling dissatisfied with their therapy or therapist because they expected too much. Their goals may be unrealistic. Their feelings from the past may be too strong to deal with in a short period of time. You may need to work on your own with what you have learned in therapy for several months, or longer, maybe even for the rest of your life. That's why a good therapist doesn't solve your problems but gives you tools so that you can learn to cope on your own as you face the other stresses and difficult transitions that life deals out.

If you feel disappointed about the limitations of your therapist or the therapy itself, discuss these issues during your counseling sessions. A competent, supportive therapist will not be afraid to look at his or her role in your disappointment. It's important for you to gauge your own expectations as well. Were they realistic? Did the therapist promise you something that wasn't delivered? Do you feel that the time has arrived to end your therapy? Do you need the continuing support? If so, make your needs and feelings known. As the consumer in this process, you are entitled to end therapy when you want to.

Types of Therapy

Therapy can involve work for just you, individually, or with your partner in couples therapy. Group therapy with other expectant or new moms may feel right as well. Another variation in therapy is the theoretical approach of the therapist. In cognitive-behavioral therapy, the focus is mainly on how the client thinks and views the world. The therapist may adopt an active, teaching focus, helping the client spot maladaptive thinking and replace it with more effective patterns. Emphasis is placed on the present. Interpersonal therapy is another theoretical approach, stressing the importance of positive relationships to well being. The therapist and client work together to evaluate the effectiveness of the client's current relationships and to help the client develop relationship skills. Focus is on the here-and-now, rather than on the past. Eclectic therapists use multiple techniques, adapting what works for individual clients. The approach of this book is eclectic, including cognitive-behavioral and interpersonal techniques, both having proven effectiveness. Our approach is action-oriented, based in the present, and aimed at empowering women.

Medications in the Postpartum Period

Sometimes, talk therapy alone is insufficient in tackling a woman's problems. Psychoactive medications such as anti-anxiety or antidepressant drugs may be needed to bring your body and mind back into balance. This is certainly not true for every woman. Medications should be chosen as an alternative after very careful consideration, especially during breastfeeding. These medications include several categories of drugs that may relieve symptoms of emotional problems.

Antidepressants, such as Zoloft, Lexapro, Cymbalta, and Wellbutrin, can relieve sadness, irritability, sleep and appetite problems, and intense anxiety. Anti-anxiety medications such as Xanax and Klonipin are short-term solutions to panic and anxiety. Mood-stabilizing (anti-mania) medications are Lithium, Depakote, Abilify, Lamictal, among others. Anti-psychotic drugs such as Zyprexa, Seroquel, and Resperidol can stop hallucinations and delusions as well as relieve anxiety and obsessions, allowing women to sleep. Sleep medications such as Ambien, Sonata, and Lunesta are sometimes prescribed for sleeplessness as well.

We believe that postpartum adjustment problems are caused by a combination of factors, psychological and emotional as well as hormonal and biological. Psychiatric medications can help women feel better faster, particularly when biochemistry has tipped the balance. These drugs can restore your brain chemistry to its previous balance. Treatment with these medications can work immediately, or can take days or weeks before you notice a change. The effect may be lasting or may disappear as soon as the medication wears off. The period of time you need to stay on the drug varies from medication to medication, as well as on the extent and severity of your symptoms.

We do not feel that these drugs should be considered an easy answer, particularly if you are breastfeeding. There are certainly other means to try before you try psychoactive drugs. These alternative methods include self-care, described in chapter two, and psychotherapy, explained in the first part of this chapter.

Breastfeeding is important nutritionally and psychologically for the baby, and for the role it plays in developing the mother-baby relationship. Medication is critical for some women in speeding their emotional recovery. But that fact needs to be balanced carefully against the importance of breastfeeding.

Recent research suggests that mothers may be able to take some psychoactive medications while pregnant or continuing to breastfeed their babies. The most up-to-date information on this topic is not included here, as new research involves continually evolving recommendations. Get the best information from an M.D. or D.O. who specializes in postpartum depression and anxiety, La Leche League or a knowledgeable lactation consultant, or a trusted website such as that of Dr. Thomas Hale, listed in the resources section of this book. This decision should not be hastily or carelessly made. Collect as many facts as you can. With the help of your partner and healthcare professionals, weigh the pros and cons of taking the medication or weaning earlier than you'd planned. Don't put yourself in the position of having to abandon breastfeeding if that doesn't seem like the best alternative. You should take medication only if it appears to be the sole route to recovery you haven't yet tried, if you're in a life-threatening situation in which medication seems to be the only answer (such as if you're suicidal) or your therapist and medical care provider deem it necessary for your recovery.

When should you explore the use of psychoactive drugs? If you're working diligently on a self-care plan, as outlined in this book, and still don't feel better within two to three weeks, you may want to explore medication as an alternative. If you're committed to breastfeeding your baby, you will want to try psychotherapy before medication, except in the most extreme cases when there is a risk to the life of mother or baby.

Many women find medication to be a useful aid to psychotherapy and self-care. Sometimes the physical symptoms of depression, agitation, panic, or sleep disturbance can be so strong that you can't focus on your self-care plan, even with the help of a therapist. Turning to medication does not mean that you are giving up or that you have failed. You are not becoming a drug addict, nor are you relying on the medication to fix everything for you. In some cases, medication can lift the fog that prevents you from doing what you need to do to take care of yourself. It's not a magic bullet; it doesn't simply make everything better. What it can do is give you enough symptom relief so that you can actually use the resources you have to help yourself. Instead of feeling overwhelmed with fatigue or caught up in obsessive thoughts, you can begin to think clearly again. When you can calm down, get some rest, or see the bright side of your world again, you can get on with the business of your recovery. In such cases, medication can be a real lifesaver.

Many therapists—especially psychiatrists—may view emotional problems, especially postpartum, as primarily biological in nature. These helping professionals are likely to recommend or prescribe psychoactive medication fairly often. Many other therapists view emotional difficulties as largely due to psychological, or life stress, causes. Knowing where your therapist stands on this issue can help you evaluate his or her recommendation that you begin to take medication for symptom relief.

In most states, psychoactive medications can only be prescribed by medical doctors, physician assistants, and nurse practitioners in most states. Psychologists, social workers, and other types of counselors usually only offer psychotherapy. If your therapist is not an M.D. or D.O., he or she will need to work in consultation with a psychiatrist or another medical professional who can prescribe medication if you choose that option. In addition to psychiatrists, many family practitioners, internists, obstetrician/gynecologists, and general practitioners may prescribe psychoactive drugs.

Before you take any medication, however, you will want to evaluate all possible sources for your symptoms. How is your health overall? Have you ruled out alternative physical causes for your symptoms? Are you taking any other medications that could be causing you to feel this way? Many medications can cause depression, anxiety, and sleep problems. As you think about the answers to these questions, be sure to include nonprescription drugs in your consideration. Do you drink a great deal of coffee, tea, or cola, or do you eat a lot of chocolate? Caffeine can cause agitation. Do you consume aspartame regularly? Diet drinks or tea sweetened with this product may increase agitation and/or depression. Do you smoke cigarettes? You shouldn't overlook the effects of nicotine. Is your diet overloaded with processed sugar? Low blood sugar can be a culprit in mood swings. Do you drink alcoholic beverages every night in an effort to relax? Alcohol close to bedtime can actually cause increased insomnia. How healthy is your diet? Lack of nourishment or an imbalanced diet, especially if you're breastfeeding, can produce physical and emotional symptoms such as mood swings, exhaustion, and panic or agitation. Are there any other medications which you take that could have side effects of depression, anxiety, or sleeplessness? Talk with your care provider about any medications you are taking, to make sure they are not causing or worsening your symptoms. You should also ask about interactions.

When Drugs Are the Only Choice

There are several postpartum clinical conditions for which medication is absolutely required. The first of these is psychosis. When a person becomes psychotic, there is a definite biochemical basis for his or her symptoms. Medication is the required treatment. It's crucial not to delay if a woman is exhibiting psychotic symptoms, (i.e., if she's having hallucinations, hearing voices, or is otherwise out of touch with reality) for there is a definite risk to the safety of the woman and her infant if proper treatment is not given.

Likewise, postpartum mania requires medication. Again, there is a biological cause for mania, the symptoms of which include extreme agitation, seemingly boundless energy despite little or no sleep, and the inability to follow one task through to completion before turning to another project. If left untreated, mania can quickly escalate into psychosis. If someone you know is experiencing any psychotic or manic symptoms (as described in chapter eight) help them to get immediate medical attention.

As mentioned earlier, women with postpartum psychosis or mania will have to discontinue breastfeeding because of the medicines prescribed for these conditions. Fortunately there are many additional ways to nurture your child including holding them, smiling at them, singing and speaking to them and bottle feeding with tenderness. Once you feel better, more opportunities to bond positively will arise. In the meantime, do what you must to get better for yourself and your baby.

11

Putting Your Postpartum Plan Together

If you have begun practicing some of the suggestions in this book, we congratulate you. As you may have discovered, there are lots of things you can do to prevent problems as well as speed your postpartum recovery. Following the recommendations in this book can help you feel better than ever — at any time in your life. Learning to be more forgiving and accepting of yourself can go a long way toward maintaining your emotional health. Allowing friends and family to help and support you is an important lesson that can only enhance your sense of connection to others.

Nurturing your relationship with your spouse or partner will strengthen your ability to cope well together during any changes or stressful times. If you come away from reading this book with nothing more than the knowledge that you must keep your pitcher full in order to be able to give of yourself to others, we will feel that we have succeeded in what we set out to do.

You Are Not to Blame

On your postpartum emotional journey, keep reminding yourself that you are not to blame for any problems you've had along the way. There is nothing you did that caused your feelings. Postpartum depression is no more your fault than having a certain eye color. For every woman, and with each pregnancy and birth, subtle interactions between biological, psychological, and relationship factors determine that particular individual's reaction at that particular point in time. Adjustment to being a parent — or increasing your family size — is one of the most challenging stages you will ever encounter. A negative, problematic reaction is not due to personal weakness or incompetence any more than an easy adjustment is an indication of intelligence or moral fiber. Becoming depressed, anxious, or disoriented does not mean that you are a failure either as a mom or a person. But it does require you, and those who care for you, to look closely at what is happening, to sort out your symptoms, and to take whatever steps are necessary to help you recover.

Do not compare your symptoms or recovery to those of other women. Doing so can lead to more negative feelings if you see yourself as worse off or recovering more slowly. If you are still not convinced that your problems aren't your fault, you may blame yourself for not doing as well as another mom. Maybe she's a better mom, smarter, more organized, or has figured out how to do things right. Stop this kind of thinking now! The truth is the more you beat yourself up over what is happening, the worse you will feel. There is no payoff here for self-criticism. Try to accept your feelings and acknowledge the factors that influence you. Focus on your individual experience and what you need to do next. You have taken an enormous step by simply reading this book. You can feel confident that you are on the right track.

Self-Help

There are many things you can do to promote your emotional well-being. The first and most important resolution you can make is to be patient and loving toward yourself. Keep focused on the huge task you are tackling, integrating a new baby into your life. Allow yourself a learning curve. Do not criticize or blame yourself for your reactions. Show as much understanding to yourself as you would toward a treasured friend. Try to be open and honest about your feelings, whatever they are. If you feel sad, angry, frightened, frustrated, or disappointed, acknowledge your losses. Embrace your grief. But go slowly. Don't push yourself to face or do too much, too soon. Trust yourself to know when you're ready to take the next step, to clear the next hurdle, or to risk another change.

It's essential to practice self-care basics. First, take good care of your physical health. Follow a healthy eating plan, exercise three times a week if you can, and get plenty of rest. Of course, these are easier said than done. Getting plenty of rest, for instance, may mean asking family members and friends to stand in for you while you put in earplugs and burrow under the covers. Do what you have to do. Don't be afraid to ask for all the support and help you need. When you feel physically run down, take time to recharge. Don't push your body to its limit any more than it's being pushed already. Fatigue and physical exhaustion can quickly cause you to feel worse.

For your emotional health, continue to call on family and friends. Having a shoulder to cry on or someone to listen sympathetically when you are feeling down is an essential component of recovery. You will feel less alone and vulnerable. Friends can be a reservoir of strength when you feel you have none left of your own. Letting friends and family help with household or childcare responsibilities will help restore your physical and emotional reserves. Be certain to let your helpers know what you need and how you want things done. You can be sensitive to their feelings, but try to stay focused on what will be most helpful to you. Trust your instincts to know what is best for you, your baby, and your immediate family.

Professional Help

If your problems require professional help, seek out a healthcare provider who is supportive, sympathetic, and knowledgeable about postpartum difficulties. Finding the right person may take some persistence. You may have to speak with several healthcare providers before you find the one who is right for you. It's critical to your recovery that you feel comfortable with your choice. Empower yourself by learning as much as you can about your particular difficulty, causes, and alternatives for treatment. Be certain to explore all of your options. If you don't want to pursue a particular recommendation, such as taking medicine, speak up. Ask what else can be done. What will be the consequences if you don't follow this recommendation? Can you try something else first? Make an informed decision by evaluating the answers to these questions. Become actively involved in designing your treatment plan. Do not surrender your freedom and allow others to choose what happens to you.

With Help, You Can Feel Better

If your symptoms are extreme or last beyond six to eight weeks postpartum, we strongly recommend that you seek professional help. You may want to start by speaking with your obstetrician and getting his or her opinion. Your OB may want to see you for an evaluation or may refer you to a healthcare provider who specializes in postpartum clinical conditions. If you're receiving appropriate care, your symptoms should diminish within two to four weeks of beginning treatment. This does not mean that you will feel fully recovered, but you should feel at least a little better.

If you are not feeling any better after a month of treatment, discuss this with your healthcare provider. It may be that you cannot see your improvement because of what you are going through or because change is occurring too slowly for you to notice it from day to day. Ask your healthcare provider to describe the changes that he or she has observed. Likewise, ask your spouse or someone who is close to you if you seem better. Others may notice changes before you do. If you're convinced there has been some improvement, stay the course. Otherwise, refer to our recommendations in chapter ten for finding the right healthcare provider. Don't settle for someone who cannot effectively help you. Although recovery can be a slow-going process, with appropriate treatment, you will start to feel better soon.

Revising Your Life, Balancing a Baby

As you have read through this book, we hope you have found valuable advice and tools for both preventing problems and surviving your transition to becoming a parent. Many of the skills you have learned here can continue to enhance the quality of your life as your child grows. Taking better care of yourself physically and emotionally will give you more energy and enthusiasm. The better you feel, the more you will have to give. The lesson from this book is to integrate these strategies for self-care into your new life as a mother. The key to avoiding mother burnout—in other words, chronically running on empty—is to revise your life. Revising your life means finding ways that work for you to balance the needs of your baby, other loved ones, and friends with your needs. You can have a baby and have a life. You can find a style that will make motherhood work for you. You can trust that there is no right or wrong way to combine the old you with the new you—but you can define the combination that works for you. You do not have to be a mother like your mother, your best friend, or your sister-in-law. You can be the mother you want to be, on your terms. Working or staying at home, volunteer-of-the-year or slacker mom, all the power to define the mom you want to be resides within you.

If you know any real-life moms who seem to have it together, observe closely. While everyone must find their own balance on this issue, there is much to be learned from watching real people parent and still have fun too. Most moms who master the seemingly impossible act of successfully juggling a baby and life have several characteristics in common. They have their priorities straight. They persist, revising as needed. They keep juggling, redoing, and experimenting as they work to find the right balance. Finally, women who make it work are prepared to make mistakes and veer off course. They know it is just plain hard to maintain new ways of acting and thinking in the face of the stress of new parenthood.

Motherhood Reviewed — Making Motherhood Work for You

As you work through this process of feeling better, remind yourself of the need to write your own version of motherhood. Being a parent is not a Hallmark card. It's not all sunshine and flowers and little hearts. It's just plain hard work most of the time, with many wonderful moments sprinkled in to keep you going. Bear this in mind and you may feel better. Expect to have some bad days and some negative feelings. Don't expect to always feel confident and doubt-free. You are tackling one of the most important, influential jobs you will ever have. Accept that it is a difficult job, with the rewards often obscured by the daily muck and mire.

Expect parenting to be tough and full of challenges. Know that the prizes for a job well done may be small and subtle. But when you see your baby smile back at you, somehow it will all seem worthwhile. With realistic expectations of motherhood, balanced with hard-won time for you, you can feel satisfied, confident, and proud of your accomplishments as you travel through this most incredible journey of a lifetime.

About the Authors

Ann Dunnewold first became interested in the adjustment to motherhood after giving birth to her first child nearly twenty-five years ago. Ann has worked with hundreds of women, offering practical tools to help them cope with life's most difficult job: parenting. She regularly shares her expertise with health professionals through training workshops, and is an internationally recognized expert on motherhood, with mention in *NBC News/The Today Show, CBS Radio, Parents.com, Parenting, and American Baby*, among others. Her mission to help women resist the pressures of modern motherhood is evident in *Life Will Never Be The Same* and her other books: *Even June Cleaver Would Forget the Juice Box, The Motherhood Club,* and *Evaluation and Treatment of Postpartum Emotional Disorders.*

From being in the trenches of life as a mom, Ann knows first hand that self-care is essential. Without it, she would be running on empty with nothing to give the women who seek her help. She makes sure that yoga or racquetball, time with good friends and good books, and creative outlets such as sewing and writing are in her life more days than not. For more information on Ann or her practice, see her website at http://anndunnewold.com.

Diane Sanford has been passionate about helping women improve their emotional health since counseling her first mom twenty-two years ago. When her daughter Jessica was born shortly after this, Diane became mildly depressed from the challenges of new motherhood. Instead of practicing self-care, she struggled to cook, clean house, and host family and friends. This experience taught her to make emotional health a priority. When her daughter Rachel arrived four years later, she balanced her needs with those of her family. She had no problems which convinced her that self-care is key to healthy postpartum adjustment.

An internationally recognized expert in pregnancy and postpartum emotional health, she has appeared on radio and TV shows including *Good Morning America*. A media expert for the American Psychological Association, Diane has been interviewed for stories in *The New York Times, Washington Post, Parents, Woman's Day, Redbook,* and numerous health/parenting websites. She is Clinical Director of Mother to Mother, and has served on the Boards of Postpartum Support International, ICEA (International Childbirth Educators Association) Consultants, and Babycenter's Medical Advisors.

Diane continues to practice self-care including daily meditation, working out, time with friends, writing, and travel. She cherishes being a mom, her most important role in life. For more information about Diane, visit her website at www.drdianesanford.com.

For the latest tips and information, please visit us at
www.realmomexperts.com

References and Resources

Resources We Mention:

Acredolo, Linda, & Goodwyn, Susan. *Baby Minds: Brain-Building Games Your Baby Will Love.* New York: Bantam, 2000.

Dix, Carol. *New Mother Syndrome.* New York: Doubleday, 1985.

Dunnewold, Ann. *Even June Cleaver Would Forget the Juice Box: Cut Yourself Some Slack (and Still Raise Great Kids) in the Age of Extreme Parenting.* Deerfield Beach, FL: Health Communications, Inc., 2007.

Lerner, Harriet. *The Dance of Anger: A Woman's Guide to Changing the Patterns of Intimate Relationships.* New York: Harper Paperbacks, 2005.

McBride, Angela B. *The Growth and Development of Mothers.* New York: Harper Collins, 1981.

McGrath, Ellen. *When Feeling Bad Is Good.* New York: Bantam, 1994.

Shelton, Sandi Kahn. *Sleeping Through the Night and Other Lies: The Mysteries, Marvels, and Mayhem in the First Three Years of Parenthood.* New York: St. Martin's, 2000.

Biochemical Issues: Hormones, Medications, Diet

Northrup, Christiane. *Women's Bodies, Women's Wisdom: Creating Physical and Emotional Health and Healing.* New York: Bantam, 2006.

Ross, Julia. *The Mood Cure: The 4-Step Program to Take Charge of Your Emotions–Today* New York: Penguin, 2003.

Sichel, Deborah and Jeanne Watson Driscoll. *Women's Moods: What Every Woman Must Know About Hormones, the Brain, and Emotional Health.* New York: Harper, 2000.

Relationships/Partners:

Gottman, John M. and Julie Schwartz Gottman. *And Baby Makes Three: The Six-Step Plan for Preserving Marital Intimacy and Rekindling Romance After Baby Arrives.* New York: Crown, 2007.

Kleiman, Karen R. *The Postpartum Husband: Practical Solutions for Living with Postpartum Depression.* Philadelphia, PA: Xlibris Corporation; 2001.

Single Mothers:

Engber, Andrea and Leah Klungness. *The Complete Single Mother: Reassuring Answers to Your Most Challenging Concerns.* Cincinnati, OH: Adams Media, 2006.

Lamott, Anne. *Operating Instructions: A Journal of My Son's First Year,* New York: Anchor, 2005.

Resources We Like that Support New Moms:

www.realmomexperts.com

www.babycenter.com

Mothers & More http://www.mothersandmore.org or 630-941-3553

Mothers of Preschoolers (MOPS) www.mops.org.

MOST (Mothers of Super Twins) http://www.mostonline.org/ or 631-859-1110
and
National Organization of Mothers of Twins Clubs www.nomotc.org or 248-231-4480

National Association of Mothers' Centers http://www.motherscenter.org/ or 877-939-MOMS

Parents as Teachers National Center, Inc. http://www.parentsasteachers.org/ or 866-PAT4YOU (866-728-4968)

www.parenting.com

www.parents.com

Thomas Hale, R.Ph., Ph.D., at his website:
    http://neonatal.ttuhsc.edu/lact/

Welcome to the World of Motherhood new mom online resource.
For more information, please see link at www.realmomexperts.com

Finding Support for Postpartum Challenges:

Postpartum Progress: Together, Stronger:
    http://postpartumprogress.typepad.com/
Award-winning blog; excellent listing of resource books.

Postpartum Support International: www.postpartum.net or 800-994-4PPD

Information and referral to resources for postpartum depression/anxiety such as support groups and health professionals in your area.

American Psychological Association
http://locator.apa.org/

National Register of Health Service Provider Psychologists
http://www.findapsychologist.org/

American Association for Marriage and Family Therapy
http://www.therapistlocator.net/index.asp

National Association of Social Workers
http://www.helpstartshere.org/common/Search/Default.asp

CPSIA information can be obtained
at www.ICGtesting.com
Printed in the USA
BVHW082106100419

545223BV00002B/101/P